NATIONAL MARITIME MUSEUM

Two mid-19th century emigrants' journals

with introduction and commentary by
ANN GIFFARD

London
HER MAJESTY'S STATIONERY OFFICE

FOR MY HUSBAND, BASIL GREENHILL

© Crown copyright 1981
First published 1981
ISBN 0 11 290335 5

BY BASIL GREENHILL AND ANN GIFFARD

Westcountrymen in Prince Edward's Isle (American Association Award: Filmed: Televised) (Toronto, 1975)
The Merchant Sailing Ship: A Photographic History (Newton Abbot, 1970)
Travelling by Sea in the Nineteenth Century (London, 1972)
Women Under Sail (Newton Abbot, 1971)
Victorian & Edwardian Sailing Ships (London, 1976)
Victorian & Edwardian Ships and Harbours (London, 1978)
Victorian & Edwardian Merchant Steamships (London, 1979)

BY BASIL GREENHILL

The Great Migration: Crossing the Atlantic under Sail (HMSO, London, 1968, ISBN 0 11 881392 7 80p.)

ACKNOWLEDGMENTS

William Fulford's journal was still in the possession of a member of his family in 1945, when it was lent to the Devon historian, the late Vernon C. Boyle*. The journal of William Gliddon was published as a broadsheet by *The Western Standard* soon after the events described therein. It was copied in manuscript by Vernon C. Boyle in 1946. I would like to thank Mr. Michael Bouquet who copied out both manuscripts and brought them to our notice, together with some notes on local matters, when my husband and I were working on *Westcountrymen in Prince Edward's Isle* in 1963. I would also like to thank Dr. L. Harrison Matthews, FRS, for his comments on the natural history mentioned in the journals, and the following at the National Maritime Museum: Mr. Alan Stimson, for enlightenment on the navigational methods used, Mr. Tim Wilson (now at the British Museum) for notes on the signal flags, and Mr. Alan Pearsall and my husband, Basil Greenhill, who both helped me to find additional information about the vessels' registration and crew lists.

* See Obituary in *The Mariners' Mirror*, Vol. 40, No. 3, August 1954, Cambridge University Press.

Contents

Introduction vii
Conditions at Home 1
The Atlantic Crossing 7
Uncle Billey's Journal 14
Log Kept by William Gliddon 41
A New Life in the Wilderness 64
Appendix 1   Crew of the *Civility* 71
Appendix 2   Crew of the *Ocean Queen* 72

FIGURES

I   Map of the North American continent in the first quarter of the 19th century viii

II   Advertisement from the *North Devon Journal*, 22nd February, 1849 10

III   Map showing the North American continent in the 1870s. 68

PLATES

between 37–41
1. An Irish cabin
2. A cottage in the Isle of Skye
3. Bideford quay circa 1860
4. River Torridge at Bideford
5. The barque *Alma*
6. Northam in the 1860s
7. Appledore quay in the 1860s
8. William Yeo
9. 'Tween decks in a timber ship
10. *Ocean Queen*
11. Emigrants at dinner
12. Emigrants collecting drinking water
13. A reading class on deck
14. Tracing the vessel's progress
15. Emigrants dancing
16. Landing place on Grosse Île, 1832
17. Cholera Bay, Grosse Île
18. View of the anchorage from Telegraph Hill
19. The Valley of Death
20. The gun battery
21. Isolation hospital
22. Montmorency Falls
23. Quebec and the coves
24. A bateau
25. The steamer *Great Britain*
26. Settlers building a house
27. White pines, Prince Edward Island
28. Forest in Prince Edward Island
29. A bush farm near Chatham, Ontario
30. Homestead in Prince Edward Island

Introduction

The two diaries which follow seemed worth publishing because they are unsensational accounts by emigrants who described their daily life in the vessels in which they sailed from the day of their departure until their safe arrival in Quebec. The two experiences are remarkably similar and although much has been written of the horrors of crossing the Atlantic under sail in the 19th century – particularly of the horrors suffered by the Irish – the vast majority of passages must have been like these, uncomfortable but humdrum. It is instructive to place these diaries in their context – the peak middle years of the period 1820–70. During these years the various Passenger Vessel Acts gradually improved the lot of the emigrants and prevented the worst abuses which had taken place earlier. Towards the end the steamship had virtually taken over from the sailing ship. In order to understand, to begin to imagine oneself in the position of these people who took part in the greatest migration – to date – of all time, it is necessary to ask three questions:

What were conditions like at home which led so many thousands to emigrate?

What was the Atlantic crossing like?

What was it like to make a new start in the vast, almost empty wilderness of North America?

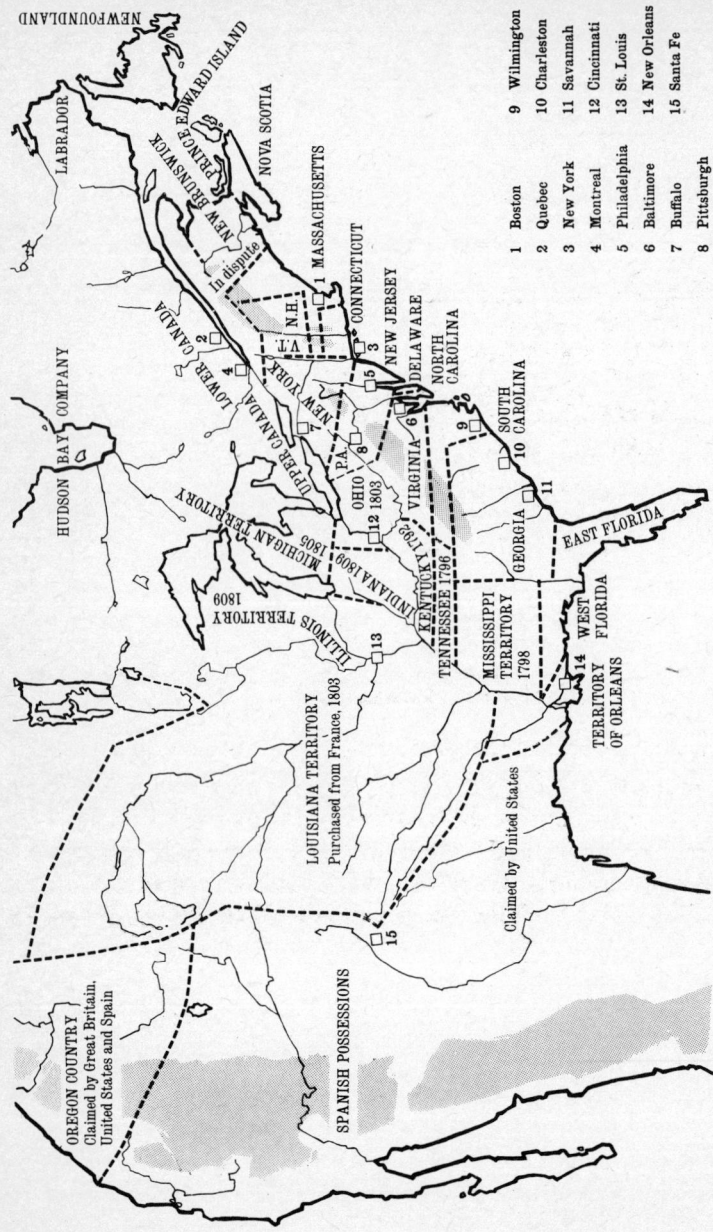

Figure 1 Map showing the settlement of the North American continent during the first quarter of the 19th century with the main inhabited areas on the eastern seaboard. (National Maritime Museum)

Conditions at Home

Since the Great Migration took place during the last century it is near enough in time for most of us to have a vivid picture of every day life and there are plenty of eye-witness accounts. The illustration which shows the interior of a cottage in the Isle of Skye (Plate 2) may seem an extreme case but there was a great deal of rural poverty in England, too. William Cobbett described his John Plodpole with 'his handful of fire and his farthing or half-farthing rushlight'.[1] Parson Hawker, living at Morwenstow in North Cornwall from 1834 onwards, wrote: 'they are crushed down, my poor people, ground down with poverty, with a wretched wage'.[2] As the century wore on the descriptions become more specific. In the 1860s the village of Halberton, near Tiverton, was described thus:

> 'The general sanitary condition of the village was very bad. Picturesque as they were externally, many of the peasant's cottages were unfit for the housing of pigs. Pools of stagnant water stood in many parts of the parish ... The whole village was badly drained, open sewers ran through it frequently trickling down from the cottages into the village brook, from which cattle slaked their thirst and the villagers and their children often drank.'[3]

As late as 1874, F. G. Heath visited the home of a Somerset man of 60:

> 'I had to stoop to get into this habitation of an English

[1] *The Political Register.*
[2] *The Vicar of Morwenstow,* S. Baring-Gould, 1949.
[3] *British Rural Life and Labour,* F. G. Heath, 1911.

agricultural labourer. The total length of the miserable hut was about seven yards, and its height measured to the extreme point of the thatched roof, about ten feet; the height of the walls, however, not being so much as six feet. From the top of the walls was carried up to a point the thatched roof, there being no transverse beams or planks. In fact had there been any I could not have stood upright in this hovel. There was, of course, no second floor to the place and the one tiny floor was divided in the middle into two compartments each about three yards square; one used for a bedroom and the other for a sitting-room.'[1]

Seventy years earlier, Arthur Young wrote of one of the reasons for this rural poverty:

'by nineteen out of twenty Enclosure Acts the poor are injured, in some grossly injured ... The poor in these parishes may say, and with truth, "Parliament may be tender of property; all I know is, I had a cow, and an Act of Parliament has taken it from me." '[2]

Not only their cows, but they also lost their gleaning rights, the possibility of growing a few vegetables, of collecting firewood. Cobbett, again, in 1824 wrote of the Industrial Revolution and the decline of cottage industries:

'The profit of a small farm received a great addition from the fruit of the labours of knitting, spinning and the like; but when these were taken away by the lords of the loom ... the little farm itself did not offer a sufficiency of means to maintain a considerable family.'[3]

Times were bad from the end of the Napoleonic Wars and through the 1830s, with spasmodic riots and rick-burning across the country. In 1815 there were riots to prevent the exportation of grain from Bideford and in 1831, Thomas Chanter, a prosperous shipowner of that little port wrote in a letter to his agent in Canada:

[1] *The English Peasantry*, F. G. Heath, 1874.
[2] *Inquiry into the Propriety of applying Wastes to the Better Maintenance or Support of the Poor.* 1801.
[3] *The Political Register.*

This country is in a very disturbed state and very little business doing – riots have prevailed lately in Bristol and on Sunday last the Mob burnt down the Mansion House in Queen Square and 30 houses, also the Bishop's palace, the Gaol and Bridewell and the Treadmill and a great many people were burnt and killed.[1]

The prospective emigrant had little to lose and, to many, loneliness in the North American wilderness would not seem either important or unfamiliar. In 1800 the Reverend Richard Warner described *A Walk Through some of the Western Counties of England*:

> 'I departed from Bideford and took the Kilkhampton road. Fortunately it happened to be market day at the former place otherwise I must inevitably have been again lost in the abominable and intricate roads of North Devon. From those who were going to attend this weekly day of public barter, who frequently ride eighteen or twenty miles for that purpose, I obtained directions through a country wild, desolate, and unpicturesque to Kilkhampton; without a single object to interest or amuse for the distance of two or three and twenty miles.'[2]

The Atlantic itself was familiar to westcountrymen who had fished in North American coastal waters since the late 16th century. The sailing vessels to be seen at Bideford Quay (Plate 3) on market day were almost as familiar to the people from the inland villages as to the townspeople. Emigration from the westcountry was not a new idea. R. D. Brown in a paper for the Devonshire Association, writing of settlement in New England before 1650 states that '95% of emigrants came from coastal villages or parishes near a coastal town'. The *North Devon Journal* carried numerous advertisements for emigrant vessels, some of which listed agents in towns as far afield as Okehampton and Tavistock. It reported in 1831:

> such is the prevailing rage for emigration, that a female who had given birth to a child but three days before, would not be

---

[1] The Port Hill papers in the Public Archives of Prince Edward Island, quoted in *Westcountrymen in Prince Edward's Isle*, Basil Greenhill & Ann Giffard, 1975.
[2] *A Walk through some of the Western Counties of England*, the Rev Richard Warner, 1800.

persuaded by the most urgent entreaties ... to remain behind for another season.[1]

The *North Devon Journal* complains:

> Many of those persons who had thus expatriated themselves are respectable farmers and their families carry with them very considerable property, thus transferring their property, their talents and their influence to another land.'[2]

These were the sort of people who might have studied the *Colonization Circular* which was published by Her Majesty's Colonial Land and Emigration Commissioners in the spring of every year. This 'useful little pamphlet' ...

> contains the names and duties of the emigration offices in the ports of the United Kingdom and in the Colonies – the cost of passage to the various colonies – a statement of the demand for labour – the rate of wages, and the price of provisions in each colony – an explanation of disposal of Crown lands – the privileges granted to naval and military settlers – the victualling scale on board ship – an abstract of the Passengers Act, and other valuable particulars'.[3]

A letter written by a young man living in a North Devon village in 1845 to his uncle who had already settled in Prince Edward Island, Canada, says it all in a nutshell:

> I am thinking of trying America as there is nothing here to look to for a living for the inhabitants is so thick and Labour is so dead there is nothing going on ...
> an if ever I come to America I think it will be next Summer for I am thinking then to take a wife an after people get settled it is a great Difficulty of removing again ... the young woman I entend to make my wife has got a brother on the Island an he is Doing very well ...[4]

[1] *North Devon Journal*, 14 April, 1831.
[2] *ibid.*
[3] *Illustrated London News*, July 6, 1850.
[4] The Port Hill papers, quoted in *Westcountrymen in Prince Edward's Isle*, Basil Greenhill & Ann Giffard, 1975.

It is easy to see that with 'nothing going on' at home, with relatives in North America reporting that they were 'Doing very well', there was every reason for emigrating if one could scrape together the money for a passage in the steerage. Amongst the passenger-brokers of Liverpool 'the competition

> in this trade is very great, and fares accordingly vary from day to day, and even from hour to hour, being sometimes as high as £5 per passenger in the steerage, and sometimes as low as £3 10s.'[1]

£3 10s. was not a high price for the respectable North Devon farmers and their families but for a labourer with a wage of 7/6d (37½p) a week it was an impossible dream. Sometimes help came from friends and relatives.

> 'Through Liverpool alone, near upon a Million sterling, in small drafts, varying from £2 or £3 to £10 each, are annually forwarded from America, for poor persons in Ireland, to enable them to emigrate; and the passage money of many thousands, in addition, is paid in New York.'[2]

Many Emigration Societies were also set up on this side of the Atlantic. There was such a one at Petworth in Sussex under Lord Egremont's patronage during the years 1832–37.[3] Lord Egremont and other local landlords paid £10 for each emigrant to provide the whole of the passage money and in addition the Poor Rates met a £5 allowance for outfitting each person. Many parishes assisted because it was cheaper to send the poor away than to have them, so to speak, 'always with us' at £9 a year in the workhouse, or at £12 a year on highway relief. Later in the century the Unions helped. The Royal Commission on Agriculture learned in 1881 that 700,000 people had emigrated with aid from the National Union of Agricultural Labourers.[4] Many of the Irish were shipped off by their landlords, as it were into outer space, a Final Solution before that terrible phrase had been coined.

There was then a finality about emigration and few who took part in the Great Migration ever expected to see their native soil

[1] *Illustrated London News*, July 6, 1850.
[2] *ibid.*
[3] *The Great Migration*, Edwin C. Guillet, 1937.
[4] *The Secret People*, E. W. Martin, 1954.

again. For this reason the departure of an emigrant vessel was always noted in the local papers and in 1831 when the *Apollo*, *Calypso* and *Bacchus*, bound respectively for New York, St Andrews and Montreal, weighed anchor at Bideford, some 5000 persons lined the quay and bridge to wave farewell (Plate 4).[1] One fact alone made possible the cheap passage of vast numbers of emigrants. This was the arrival in England of vessels laden with timber from Canada. The still sparsely inhabited North American continent was self-sufficient as far as food and most other natural resources were concerned: such manufacturing industries as were needed were rapidly established. Some equipment for the expanding Canadian shipbuilding industry, some cattle and horses for breeding were taken over, also whisky and rum, otherwise the westward bound vessels would have been almost empty had it not been for their human cargo.

[1] *North Devon Journal*, 14 April, 1831.

The Atlantic Crossing

The accounts in the Journals which follow differ in many ways from descriptions of emigrant vessels which left the crowded port of Liverpool, where conditions were much more chaotic, the masters were not so well-known, the crews not so much family affairs. There you had to take what you could get from the emigration office. Many people were cheated. Not only was there an inspection at the Medical Inspector's Office but during the tow down the Mersey there was a roll-call of passengers and a rigorous search for stowaways which might take several hours while the passengers were kept standing on deck. Neither of these procedures are mentioned in our journals.

Early April was the usual time for the first crossings of the year – *Civility* and *Ocean Queen* would hope to make two crossings in each direction before the winter, in a particularly favourable year they might make three. The earliest possible departure was also of great advantage to the emigrant, giving him the maximum amount of time to settle in before the onslaught of snow and ice.

Both writers were travelling steerage and a few weeks earlier the space in which they were to live for more than six weeks would have been filled with timber, as it would be again for the return voyage. (Plate 9) But advertisements of emigrant ships made a point of the comfort and convenience of passengers. (Figure 2) In 1849 Richard Heard's barques *Devonia*, *Secret* and *Civility* were described as:

> 'very substantial and fast sailing Ships, (*they*) carry experienced Commanders, are very roomy in the twixt decks, and can afford accommodation (in each Vessel) for about Ten Cabin

Passengers. A more desirable opportunity for individuals and families about to emigrate cannot be offered, as only a limited number of passengers will be taken in each Vessel, which will very much increase the comfort of the passengers.'[1]

The accommodation (except for the Cabin passengers) was communal in every sense – men, women and children all together in their family groups. The damp, unheated living quarters gave William Fulford and many of the other passengers in the *Civility* sore throats. Both writers report the piercing cold. But, provided the vessel was well-ordered, as *Civility* and *Ocean Queen* undoubtedly were, life on board was tolerable by the standards of the times – certainly no worse, except for those who were sick, than life in the type of cottages many of the emigrants had come from. It is true that the weather could make it more alarming and it was certainly noisy. One is apt to forget that a wooden ship is constantly creaking, sailors run across the deck to work the ship even in the small hours, the rigging rattles, the sails make a great flapping noise.

In a day or two most people had got their sea-legs and we can see from these two journals that it was very largely up to the passengers to make themselves comfortable and to provide their own amusement and instruction. 'Uncle Billie' was kept busy giving out religious tracts and to the end of the voyage he held prayer meetings at 7 o'clock every evening. Life in the *Ocean Queen* was more light-hearted with a concert and dancing. The principal amusement, common to both vessels, was Neptune's Court, held when they crossed the Banks. These well-known Crossing the Line ceremonies were also held in many other areas such as the Tropics, the Strait of Gibraltar and even far into the interior of Canada a thousand miles from the Ocean. Such ceremonies are recorded as early as 1756 and were for the purpose of raising money for the sailors so that they could buy 'wine and good cheer' when the ship got into port.[2]

Daily life on board was very much like life in a commune – the crew entertained the passengers: the Captain could call on the

---

[1] *North Devon Journal*, 22nd February, 1849.
[2] See note by Malcolm Macleod in *The Mariner's Mirror*, Vol 53, No. 3, Aug. 68, Cambridge University Press.

passengers for help, both social and technical. Apart from keeping watch during foggy weather, cooking, doing some sewing for the Mate, Uncle Billie was asked to collect all the children and teach them to read and spell. By implication the other passengers and crew were literate and able to read his religious tracts. When the jibboom was carried away the craftsmen set to work making a new one. Five days later many of the sailors and tradesmen passengers were helping to place the new jibboom in the vessel. Craftsmanship of this kind has been lost and to-day's tall ships must go to an expensive shipyard to be repaired.

Both Captains were friendly with their steerage passengers, not only with the cabin passengers. William Gliddon played draughts with Captain Dart, who also showed him *Ocean Queen's* course plotted on the chart. He learned about ships' signals and the meaning of different flags. A Captain was also responsible for hygiene and in fine weather would order a general clean-up and airing of clothes and bedding. Many were presented with a piece of silver by their grateful passengers. Captain Dart received a testimonial in the form of a letter when *Ocean Queen* reached Quebec.

From the evidence of these journals it would appear that both Captains were navigating by the old method of latitude sailing, (used universally before methods of determining longitude at sea were developed in the late 18th century) that is, estimating their course and distance made good each day and correcting their position by a latitude check at noon by an observation of the sun whenever this was possible. This confirms reports of the low standards of navigation in certain vessels at this time and shows why the Government introduced compulsory examinations for masters and mates in the Mercantile Marine Act, 1850. Provisioning was largely conditioned by whichever of the Passenger Acts happened to be current. The *Vittoria* advertisement of 1849 states:

'Passengers, if required may be victualled on the Ship's account, or find themselves. A cook will be provided.'[1]

In fact, with less than one hundred passengers it was not a statutory

[1] *North Devon Journal.*

EMIGRATION

To Quebec, Montreal, Upper and Lower Canada, Prince Edward Island, &c.

THE following well-known first class Ships will sail from Bideford and Bristol, on or about the 2nd day of April next, (weather permitting,) taking Goods and Passengers.

The Barque 'DEVONIA,' 950 Tons Burthen, will sail from Bristol for Quebec and Montreal direct.

The Barque 'SECRET,' 600 Tons Burthen, will sail from Bideford for Quebec and Montreal direct.

The Barque 'CIVILITY,' 450 Tons Burthen, will sail from Bideford for Prince Edward Island and Nova Scotia.

All of the above vessels are well known as very substantial and fast sailing Ships, carry experienced Commanders, are very roomy in the twixt decks, and can afford accommodation (in each Vessel) for about Ten Cabin Passengers. A more desirable opportunity for individuals and families about to emigrate cannot be offered, as only a limited number of passengers will be taken in each Vessel, which will very much increase the comfort of the passengers.

Every accommodation possible will be given to the passengers, and no expense spared to make them comfortable during the voyage.

For particulars, apply to Mr. R. HEARD, Merchant, Bideford.

Each of the above Vessels will return direct to Bideford.

R. HEARD takes this opportunity to inform his friends and the public generally, that he has on sale at his yards in Bideford, at reduced prices, Quebec and St. John's Yellow and Red Pine, White Lake Oak, Birch Logs of very excellent quality and large dimensions which have been carefully selected, red and white Baltic Deals, well-seasoned Board and Plank of every description; also Laths, Staves, &c.

Bideford, February 16th, 1849.

Figure II Advertisement from the North Devon Journal, 22nd February, 1849.

requirement to carry a 'seafaring person to act as passenger's cook, and also with a proper cooking apparatus.'[1] In 1851, in another advertisement Richard Heard stated:

> Provisions supplied weekly to each passenger – $2\frac{1}{2}$ lbs of bread or biscuit, 1 lb wheaten flour, 5 lbs oatmeal, 2 lbs rice, $\frac{1}{2}$ lb sugar, $\frac{1}{2}$ lb treacle or molasses, 2 oz Tea, 21 quarts of good water.
> For terms of passage, which will be Much Lower than is charged by any other vessel including similar comforts and provisions apply to the owner.[2]

There was a certain amount of improvisation. After only ten days out, the *Civility* 'caught some soft water today, which is very good, the water on board is getting very bad', and 'one of our sailors with a hook and line caught a large codfish $17\frac{3}{4}$ lbs'. William Gliddon's only mention of food, except when they were unable to cook because of the storm is that 'I made bread today which is allowed to be the best on board'. One must conclude that food on the *Ocean Queen* was unexceptional.

One of the very real pleasures of crossing the Atlantic in a sailing vessel, as opposed to one of the latter-day liners, was the feeling of closeness to Nature. These were country people and they noted natural phenomena with interest and delight, Mother Carey's chickens, stormy petrels, a large baulk of wood completely covered with barnacles, porpoises or sea-pigs, a whale and a grampus. Every vessel seen was noted and of course the ones which were homeward bound would carry news of the outward bound vessels to their home ports. These were long voyages. It was possible to reach Quebec in under thirty days, twenty-one days was a record, forty-two the average to westward, but both these vessels were beset by storms. The first sight of land – which 'brought joy to every heart' was Cape Breton, thirty-seven days out for *Civility*, thirty-nine for *Ocean Queen*.

There were, of course, very real dangers. The emigrant ship, the barque *John*, ran on the rocks soon after leaving Plymouth in 1855. The master and crew, who were drunk, abandoned the passengers.

---

[1] *Illustrated London News*, July 6, 1850.
[2] *North Devon Journal*, 13 February 1851.

Or, the vessel might have to return as in the case of the *Marina* in 1835, which in the words of her owner, Thomas Chanter of Bideford:

> sailed early and off Ireland sprang a leak – and but for the number of Passengers she would have gone down with them – I much fear she will lose her two voyages by the accident.[1]

In this case the passengers manned the pumps so that the crew could sail the *Marina* back to her home port. And sometimes, despite all precautions such as the safety lamp with a padlock so that it could not be opened by passengers, which is now in the Emigration Gallery in the National Maritime Museum, there was fire at sea. However, the only tragedy in these two voyages was the death of Isaac Harvey – a typical industrial accident.

Perhaps the most unfortunate disaster of all was the presence of disease on board an emigrant vessel. To try to prevent the entry of cholera into Canada, a quarantine station was established in 1832 on Grosse Île, about thirty miles below Quebec.[2] Here all vessels proceeding up the St Lawrence were obliged to stop. A battery of three guns, which remain in position to this day, was set up to command the passage between Grosse Île and the southern shore of the St Lawrence, by a company of the 32nd Regiment under a Captain Alderson. A staff house, two large sheds for immigrants, a bakery and a hospital were also built, but for some years there was no wharf so stores and passengers alike, the sick, the dying and the dead, had to be landed on the south shore of the island where the deep water is. Not far out the tides are very strong and when there is a wind adverse to the tide a very nasty sea rapidly builds up. Waiting vessels must have had a most uncomfortable time.

The hospital soon proved inadequate and the summer before William Fulford wrote his journal, the summer of the great cholera disaster, there had been queues of vessels, performing their quarantine but unable to land their sick.[3]

---

[1] The Port Hill papers, letter to William Ellis, 28th April, 1835.
[2] See 'Events Leading up to and the Establishment of the Grosse Île Quarantine Station', Chas. A Mitchell, DVM, LL.D, FRSC, *Medical Services Journal Canada*, Vol. XXIII. No. 11, December, 1967.
[3] *The Great Hunger*, Cecil Woodham Smith, London, 1962.

Grosse Île is always described as 'beautiful', as indeed it is, and this adds poignancy to the interest of the place. To visit it today, it is necessary to obtain a permit from the Ministry of Agriculture & Fisheries in Ottawa, who use it on occasion as an animal quarantine station and who, in spring, run a training course there for veterinary students. One man, born and brought up on Grosse Île, M. Masson, lives there as caretaker, apparently immune to the ghosts. There remain some buildings, which include a huge iron boiler for fumigating clothes, a guard-house built to prevent those in quarantine from crossing the narrow neck of land into the non-infected area, two white wooden Churches, one Roman Catholic, the other Protestant, and the 1850s hospital, a long, low shed used during World War II as a chicken house. 120 feet above the river on Telegraph Hill is a granite cross, placed there in 1909 by the Ancient Order of the Hibernians in America, in memory of the thousands of Irish immigrants who died on Grosse Île. Below, in a small valley, the only place where the soil was deep enough to bury the dead, is a long row of plain wooden crosses, tip-tilted above the vegetation, the wild michaelmas daisies and the golden rod. Under the trees is another monument bearing the names of six doctors who died of cholera or typhus, and the famous inscription:

> In this secluded spot lie the mortal remains of 5,294 persons, who, flying from pestilence and famine in Ireland in the year 1847, found in America but a grave.'

Nearby is a beautiful little sandy bay, chillingly named Cholera Bay, where William Gliddon saw the people 'washing and scrubbing like fun'. Today, unvisited by tourists, it remains a travel brochure photographer's dream.

There are no distress stories in the *North Devon Journal* of troubles at Grosse Île, as there would have been if these little westcountry vessels had not been well run and their passengers 'decent and healthy'. Perhaps these two journals will redress the balance a little, away from the many horrific accounts of the sufferings of emigrants from the larger ports.

Uncle Billey's Journal

March 31st 1848

A Journal and Memorandum of Incurring Relative to William Fulford in leaving Old England, North of Devon and Residence and Birthplace, viz, Southwood House situated in Buckland Brewer village (Plate 6) near Bideford, also my dear Brothers and Sisters, Relatives and intimate Acquaintances.

I had to bid farewell on Friday the 31st at 11 o'ck in the forenoon, and arrived at Bideford in the afternoon with the remainder of my Relatives until the 5th of April on Wednesday morning at half past 5 o'ck in the morning on board the ship *Civility* who left Bideford Quay (Plate 4) at 7 o'ck in the morning and sail'd down the River to Appledore opposite Graysand Hills and cast anchor for the night where I had to bid farewell to all my dear Relatives and to give vent to my natural and painful feelings and to uncomfortable and inconveniences of domestic life, attending on Board a Vessel.

[The barque *Civility* (Plate 5) was built at Vernon river, Prince Edward Island, by Thomas Richards, who signed the Builder's Certificate for George Heard of Charlottetown, P.E.I. She was registered there in 1842, 247 tons, 94.6 x 20.2 x 15.5. In May 1843 she was transferred to Bideford, England, as owned 64/64ths by Richard Heard. During ten years of Heard ownership she made many Atlantic crossings and once made the spring passage to Charlottetown in twenty-three days. In 1848 she made two round-trips, leaving for the second one from Plymouth on August 8th. The following February she was advertised as sailing from Bideford for Prince Edward Island and Nova Scotia, taking Goods and Passengers on or about 2nd day of April. We know she cleared P.E.I. for the Miramichi on June 14th. She returned to England and sailed again from Bideford on 19th August, entering at Charlottetown on Sept 17. Three days later she cleared, again for the Miramichi, and was back in Bideford on November 12th.

She was sold in 1852 to Frederick Storey, a merchant of Hartlepool and immediately re-registered there. She was presumably used as a collier. On 29th November, 1853, she was again re-registered at Hartlepool, now brig-rigged and without her figurehead of a woman. In February 1855 she was sold to her master, Sherinton Foster, who the following month sold 32/64ths to another Hartlepool master mariner, George Graham. She does not appear in the first issue of the Mercantile Navy List in 1857 and the assumption must therefore be made that she was lost or broken up in late 1855 or early 1856.]

At 8 o'ck at night me and brother Bat and wife and children retired to our berths to rest, all in good health. Thank God for it, but I did not sleep all the night.

Thursday the 6th:

Blessed be God, I feel I am safe anchor'd in Jesus. In Him is my hope and joy and rest. I rose at my usual hour 6 o'ck, prepared for Devotion, found a throne of Grace accessible, my soul drawn out, and prayer to God a refreshing season. From his presence I can say all is well with me, and in the right way to the heavenly and earthly Port to which we are bound.

At 7 o'ck Mr Heard came on board and gave orders to the Captain to go over the Bar, also the Custom House Officers and Pilotmen came on Board, and while they were performing their offices and hauling the anchors we had breakfast on our temporary table, viz. on our chest and box, and to despatch it as quickly as possible.

[Richard Heard, first described as a joiner of Bideford, began to dabble in vessel property in the early 1830s. In the early 1840s he entered the timber, shipbuilding and emigrant trades with the *Civility* and the *Em B. Heard* (also built in the Island under the supervision of George Heard). In 1840, Richard sent his son

William to Charlottetown to act as his agent. George, who was apparently Richard's brother, returned to Bideford about this time. The family prospered and William Heard oversaw the building and financing of over forty vessels which were sent home to be sold by Richard and George, or to be retained and operated by them from Bideford. William Heard also set up a store in Charlottetown. He placed many advertisements relating to the *Civility* in 'The Islander': for 'A large Assortment of DRY GOODS', for '40,000 Bridgwater bricks' and for a 'large and elegant assortment of French and British Millinery' for his wife's Showroom. He became one of the Island's leading inhabitants and died in the 1890s in Charlottetown after fifty years' residence there.

The Captain is not mentioned by name in this Journal except as 'Uncle John, the Captain', to whom little Alice had become 'the pet' (Friday, 14th April) but *Civility's* Statutory Registration documents in Bideford Custom House have the notation that 'Jn. Bale' was appointed her master on 22nd May, 1846. He was still shown as master in the relative Agreement for the voyage from Bideford towards Quebec March 1848, now in the Public Records Office. These Westcountry vessels were run very much as family affairs and there are three other Bales in the crew list for this particular voyage (See Appendix 1). Ed Bale, the cook, was most probably a brother since like John Bale he was born at Alphington. John Bale appeared in *The Islander* newspaper as master for both *Civility's* 1849 voyages to Charlottetown. The 1851 Census shows John Bale, Master Mariner, aged 39, living at 36 Irsha Street, Appledore, with his wife Mary, three sons and three daughters.]

Between eight and nine in the morning we were Piloted over the Bar to encounter the Boisterousness of the winds and the waves of the Atlantic Ocean; and through the Sailing and Rolling of the vessel we and all the passengers were Sea-sick, except John Collins. He was not sick at all. He was very kind and serviceable to us in administering to our wants, as I and Brother Bat and Prudence and Children retired to our Berths, there to lye with our heads out over to throw up the contents of the stomach and we could not take nor make much spoil with our food.

The vessel made a favourable way through a strong Northwest wind, 7 or 8 miles an hour, so that we bid farewell to our dear

England, for we lost sight of it about 3 o'ck in the afternoon.

7th Friday morning:

I bless God I have slept well tonight and find myself in good health and quite freed from sea-sickness and not in the least giddy in my head. I believe that my remedy was by drinking a little best brandy yesterday. I have been on the top deck today and walked from the steerage to the boughsprit the leeward and the windward side of the vessel, and gazed on the mighty Western Ocean, to adore the Wisdom and Power of God that created and spread the flowing seas abroad and set its bounds that it cannot pass over to cover the earth.

Favourable weather today, sun and sky bright and clear. The wind is a little more East and not quite as strong. Bat and Wife and children are a little better in their seasickness today, but when on their legs they stagger like drunken men, and when laying down they are like dead lumps, except Edward who is entirely recovered: so me and Edward and John Collins is the best on board.

Sailing today is not quite so smart about 5 miles an hour and the vessel lurches and rolls from side to side a great deal.

Saturday 8th:

My sleep not so well. The night passed in consequence of the vessel rolling and tossing about like a little boat, towards the morning. But when I awoke the Lord was present with me, and all my ransomed power was taken up with God for His Glory and the spiritual prosperity of his Church below and the salvation of the apostate race of Adam, especially those on board: I with them as I lay in my Birth. I thought of my dear Brothers and Sisters, relations and acquaintances I had left behind, and the spiritual and domestic blessings I had enjoyed with them in dear old England.

Rather rough and rainy today, yet the wind is fair, and the vessel making way fair for the port. We got in sight of a Brig in the forenoon and passed her in the evening. Bat and the children remain sick except Edward; all the passengers remain sick except John Collins, but still, getting better.

Sunday 9th:

I have still reason to praise God in sparing me and in good health another Sabbath to enter upon its duties and priveleges; the first upon the mighty deep. I thought early this morning of my dear native chapel of my little hill miser (?) where I have so many times past, alone by myself in the spirit of faith and prayer, held communion with my God, and realised so much of his glorious Presence, and with my dear parteners and comrades in the bonds of faith and love and fellowship of saints: Titus, Mr Burnard, Robert Squire and all who I thought were praying for me and the rest on board at the 7 o'ck prayer meeting; and surely the Lord heard and answered my prayer, for my birth was as the House of God and the gate of Heaven to me.

['Mr. Burnard' was possibly one of the three sons of the great Bideford merchant and shipowner, Thomas Burnard, four times mayor of Bideford, died 1823. The voyage of Thomas Burnard's *Peter & Sarah* in 1818 led to the development of shipbuilding in Prince Edward Island by North Devon men, including the Heard and Yeo families. The story is told in *Westcountrymen in Prince Edward's Isle*.]

We took breakfast and afterwards I devoted a little time to reading and study, and then went on deck and conversed with the Captain respecting the Sabbath in reverence and devoting it to the Lord; and in the middle of the forenoon the Captain gave orders to all the passengers that possibly could to come on deck and assemble themselves together in front of the Cabin to unite in the service of Almighty God, when I had the satisfaction in giving out a few verses of our hymn, which begins thus –

> 'Praise ye the Lord. 'Tis good to raise
> Our hearts and voices in this praise.'

The Captain, sailors and all united in praising God. Brother Nichols engaged in prayer, all was orderly, devout and solemn. God was in our midst. Then I gave out a few verses of our hymn, and all sang. I read the 107th Psalm, engaged in prayer, and concluded the Service and distributed tracts to all present which they read. I soon found out that there were eight pius passengers on board besides myself. Seven of them were united to Mr. Thom's people, and one of them a brother Cann, a native of Langtree was a local preacher.

[The 107th Psalm, of course, contains the famous verses beginning 'They that go down to the sea in ships...' with its vivid description of seasickness. 'They mount up to the heaven, they go down again to the depths: their soul is melted because of trouble. They reel to and fro, and stagger like a drunken man, and are at their wit's end'. James Thom lived at Shebbear, a village not far from Buckland Brewer, and was one of the founders there of the Bible Christian Sect. He died in 1872.]

It was very pleasant today: the sun and sky bright and clear, the wind fair, the sea smooth, and the vessel sailing at the rate of 8 miles an hour.

Between the morning service and dinner time I had an invitation by Miss Crealock of Littleham, a Wesleyan member and a cabbin passenger to have an interview with her.[1] I embraced the opportunity. We all in the cabin improved the remainder of the time in reading and conversing on religious subjects, and it was very profitable. It was proposed to conduct Divine Service in the evening in the Cabin, so I conversed again with the Captain respecting it. He readily consented, so at 7 o'ck we again assembled for worship. Br's Cann, Nichols and Ancock gave out verses of an hymn and all sang the praises of God. We engaged in prayer and could say the best of all was God was with us.

Monday 10th:

We have had favourable weather. I slept tolerably well, and in good health, thank God. The wind rather contrary: N.W.

Bat and family, Wm. Shute and Sarah, and all the passengers are better, getting their appetite and complaining of their hunger. (Plate 11) The provisions we took with us we have found most useful, such as flour, as we can bake household bread every three days if we like for 1d. a loaf; also a pie or pudding at $^1/_2$d each. There is an excellent cast iron oven and Boiler in the Galley and it belongs solely to the Cook (Ed Bale) who is an excellent Cook.

Bat and Wm. Shute might have sold their cider at a high price, $2^1/_2$ per pint if they would have disposed of it. We found everything

---

[1] A James Crealock, shoemaker and victualler, had the Hoop Inn at Littleham. *White's Directory*, 1850.

we took most useful. Myself and Bat and all the family have still reason to express our gratitude to our kind friends at Buckland and Bideford and Northam. We pray that the Lord may restore to you fourfold for all past favours.

We had a good prayer meeting in the hold at 7 o'ck.

Tuesday 11th:

A very uncomfortable night: the ship tossing as high as mountains; the poor sailors up all night, drenched with the sea. We could not sleep for the night. Some of us were obliged to turn out from our births to fasten our chests and boxes etc., as all our utensils were rattling about. But in the midst of danger I had to cast my care on God, and could trust Him who holds the winds in his fists and the Waters in the hollow of His hands.

During the storm the gibboom of the vessel was carried away. Also the temporary galley was upset, which rolled over Robert Cann and John Baglow, who were holding on to it to save themselves against the vessel's side. It was a mercy that they were not killed. They were carried below and means applied for their recovery. We held our usual prayer meeting at 7 o'clock.

Wednesday 12th:

We had a rough night again: the wind still against us, but thank God we are all spared and preserved. Nearly all have passed their sea-sickness and all are well except Cann and Baglow. The men-passengers are building up a temporary galley and fastened it to the Cook's galley, as the cooking goes on from morning to night.

At midday we discovered a ship making towards us. She came within a gunshot. She was called the *Lady Peel* from Penzance in Cornwall.[1] There were a great many passengers.

We held our usual prayer meeting at 7 o'ck. So many of the sailors as can assemble with us. They delight to hear us in singing. I pitch and lead the tunes whilst Bat and children and all follow, so we have a general concert.

---

[1] A ship of 567 tons, built Quebec 1843 by Thos. Lee. Owned 1849 by John J. Nichols, Plymouth, voyage Plymouth – Quebec, Master, L. Luety.

Thursday 13th:

It is now a week since we were piloted over the Bar. We have encountered dangers and afflictions, but by the Lord's help, myself, Edward Fulford and John Collins are in good health and most of the passengers are passing their sea-sickness. Cann and Baglow remain still unwell.

During the past week the vessel has made 5 or 6 hundred miles. Today we have seen numbers of porpoises or sea-pigs.[1] Prayer meeting as usual, 7 o'ck.

Friday 14th:

Had a good night's rest. I bless and praise God for all his mercies. Wind still fair. Vessel sailing at the rate of 6 or 7 miles an hour. Myself, Bat, Prudence and the children have thus far on the voyage been accommodated in the day time in the cabin, and little Alice is become the pet with the cabin passengers, and often takes her meals with them. She has become the pet of her Uncle John, the Captain, and Richard the mate and Edward Bale the Cook and most of the sailors. She can walk on the top deck from the steerage to the bough sprit, from leeward to windward equal to any on board and climb the ladders up and down the hatchways. God's presence was felt at our prayer meeting: we felt it was good to be there.

Saturday 15th:

Weather rather changeable during the night; raining today. We have seen three ships today, two outward and one homeward-bound. We caught some soft rain-water today, which is very good, as the water on board is getting very bad.

Sunday 16th:

The second Sabbath at sea. I woke this morning at my usual hour and thought on my dear Relations and Friends at Northam and the last Sabbath I spent with them in England. I felt you were all

---

[1] A general term for the smaller *cetacea* (dolphins). Unlikely to have been true Common Porpoise at this distance in the open ocean.

praying for me and all on board. Your prayers were answered. After breakfast I went from birth to birth and changed the tracts. All appeared pleased to read them. I found there were two passengers named Cann, Robert and Edward, both of them pious, Edward being a local preacher. I solicited him to prepare a sermon for the Service, but the wind was so high and the sea so rough that friend Cann was so unwell he could not conduct divine service; but we assembled in the hold, and held a prayer meeting and found it good to draw near to God. And God was immanently present: Sweeter than honey to my soul.

Monday 17th:

I have not slept much tonight in consequence of the stormy weather; however, the gale is hushed to a calm. As there is a good carpenter, a wheelwright and a ship's carpenter on board they all set to work making a new jib-boom for the vessel, and John Fulford is making a ladder for the hatchway. The vessel is still making progress. Myself, Bat and his family are under the necessity of taking medicine, but it has proved a benefit to our health. Thank God for it. Rob. Cann is restored again and John Baglow is almost recovered.

Tuesday 18th:

This morning I woke with a sore throat and tightness across my chest. I am inclined to think it is due to the changeableness of the weather and the severity of the cold and the dampness of the hold where we live, but I have applied means for my recovery. Bat, Prudence and family are well, thank God. John Baglow is still unwell, and Mrs Veal and Mrs Pasker have been sick thus far on the voyage; and as there are 56 passengers, ten of them under 14 years of age, and four infants, the Captain desired me to collect all the children that were fit for tuition and teach them to read and spell in the cabin, two or three hours a day. I readily consented. (Plate 13)

We were in company with a Brig today. She came near us. The two Captains spoke, enquiring where from and where bound for, also compared latitudes, which proved to be alike.[1] She was from Waterford bound to Quebec.

Wed. 19th:

Still suffering from my cold, but I feel it is the Lord's doing, and amongst all the things that work together for good. I have been in the cabin with the children.

Another ship passed us this evening. She was bound to England. Our Captain hoisted the British flag and hailed him, but as soon as they saw our flag they sheered off and would have nothing to say. They were sulky Yankees. She was the *Columbia*, of Bath, U. States.[2]

Thursday 20th:

Slept well tonight, but my throat is still painful and cough troublesome. I find my appetite rather delicate, which is unusual for me, but I am not surprised, as our sea-biscuits contain so much horse-bean flour, and our water is so impure that it produces indigestion. Never since I was born have I proved the value of good bread and the Western Well water at Buckland Brewer, its excellency and value until deprived by the sea voyage: still, I am reposing all my confidence in God, who can cause all things to work together for good.

John Baglow came out of bed today; however, the weather is still boisterous and against us. We have been a fortnight at sea, so shortened our voyage, a little more than a third. I have attended to the children in the cabin, also done a job of sewing for the Mate, so you will perceive that my time is improved through the course of the day and in conducting the prayer meeting in the evening. I find that the service of God is perfect freedom to our souls.

Friday 21st:

Being Good Friday, the first I ever spent on the wide Ocean. My

---

[1] The Captains were comparing latitudes as a check that they had got it right, the observed latitude being all important in this type of navigation. See page [9].
[2] There were many American vessels of this name, but none owned in Bath, Maine. Perhaps the most likely is the ship *Columbian*, built 1845 at Bath, owned John Henry, master S. Merriman.

sleep the night passed hath not been so well. I endeavoured to improve the time in contemplating the sufferings of Christ, and what Jesus bore for me. Blessed be his name, I could say.

> Jesus, my all in all thou art,
> My rest in toil, my ease in pain.
> The medicine of my broken heart,
> In war my peace, in loss my gain.
> My smile beneath the tyrant's frown,
> In shame my glory and my crown.

The vessel is making her right course. We saw, for the first time in our lives, a live Whale, about two-thirds the length of our vessel, skipping along at the rate of twenty miles an hour, spouting the water high up into the air.[1]

Saturday 22nd:

My sleep has been better, but I am still unwell, but I believe that God who afflicts my body can also heal it and restore it to health, so I trust in Him for a cure. Many of the passengers are suffering from cold. This afternoon many of the sailors and tradesmen passengers are helping to place the new jibboom in the vessel. The wind is favourable: the vessel sailing at 7 or 8 miles an hour.

Sunday 23rd:

The third Sabbath at sea, and the first Easter Sunday. I feel a little better and thank God for it. I began the day contemplating the grand scheme of Man's Redemption by the Resurrection of Jesus from the dead, and by examination I found that I enjoyed a part of the first resurrection through faith in the risen Christ. My cry is, 'O Lord, raise me into a higher state of spiritual life'. I changed tracts and found the sailors anxious to read them. I proposed to the Captain to have divine service, so the Cap. gave orders to assemble, and Bro. Ed. Cann took a text from 3rd Chap. I Ep. Peter, part verse 18, 'For Christ suffered, the just for the unjust, that he might bring us to God'. I trust the good seed was not sown in vain. We assembled again in the evening in the cabin for worship and found it good to be there. It was a good day to my soul.

[1] Possibly a Fin whale.

Monday 24th:

Very rough all night: it blew a gale of wind. As I lay awake I thought of my dear Brothers and sisters and friends in Buckland, Parkham, Bideford and Northam, and remembered them at the throne of Grace and beg that you will never forget me in prayers as long as he spared you in body. During our prayer meeting this evening I had the painful necessity of reproving the disorderly conduct of some persons, and their sinful conversation was hushed into silence and attention.

Tuesday 25th:

A rough wind; the poor sailors have had no rest for two nights. Let no persons on land envy the comforts and enjoyments of the sailors, for they have but little at sea, drenched and washed as they are, tossed about in the mighty deep. John Baglow is better, and able to attend to the care of his wife and family.

Wednesday 26th:

The rough is become smooth and favourable, and myself, Bat and Prudence, and all the children and all on board have slept tolerable mild. Myself and all the sick are restored to health and strength. Bless and praise God for it. The Lord is in our midst.

Thursday 27th:

This day three weeks the vessel sailed over the Bar and we lost sight of our dear native land. Today we have been all on deck like bees from their hives: the sun shining warm and beautiful.

Friday 28th:

Continued fine weather. I arose, engaged in my usual devotion. The best of my heart and mind was taken up with God, and the cry of the soul was 'O Lord, help me to glorify Thee, with body and soul which are Thine'. Cap. ordered a general clean-up of clothes and bedding to be brought on deck, the hold to be opened, berths to be cleaned to prevent disorder, so we were busy as bees in preparing for a rainy day. At night the weather showed signs of change, so orders were given to shorten sail so as to prepare for storm.

Sat 29th:

Very rough night. The vessel rocked like a cradle. Expected every minute to tumble out of our berths. Scarcely any sleep: sea mountains high. Crew on deck all night, each of them taking a turn at the wheel every four hours. The two pumps are at work as there is continuous need of keeping the pumps going[1], the vessel taking in so much water; so you perceive that if we have some days fine weather, at others we are kept below. But by the protection and mercy of God we are spared.

Sunday 30th:

Not so rough, with more composure and rest. We are spared to the fourth Sabbath morning on the wide ocean. The desire of my heart and prayer is:

> In holy pleasures pass away
> How sweet the Sabbath thus to spend
> In hopes of that which ne'er shall end.

The Cap. gave orders to assemble for Div. worship, so Bro. Ed. Cann our local preacher conducted service, took a text from 32nd Chap. Deut. verse 29, 'Oh, that they were wise, that they understood this, that they would consider their latter end'. I trust that the seed thus sown was as bread cast upon the waters, to be seen after many days. In the afternoon the wind rose and blew very hard. As it appeared likely to be a rough night the Cap. ordered the sailors to reef the sails. In the evening we assembled in the cabin for prayer, committing ourselves to His protecting and keeping through the coming strife.

Monday May 1st:

During the past night the wind, waves and sea was tremendous rough with torrents of rain. The females and children were screeching, and men and all exclaimed 'What can we do, we cannot lye here'. I said to Bat's boy, Ned, for we sleep together, 'Well Ned, we must get a rope and lash ourselves to our birth, or

---

[1] William Fulford was fortunate that he did not have to man the pumps himself, see page 12 & William Gliddon, Thursday 12th April.

over we must go'. However, Ned fell asleep and slept all night. I believe he could sleep on the deck, for he is as astonishing a lad to sleep as I ever knew in my life. I could not sleep, as the vessel rolled; the wind blowing all through the rigging sounded like thunder. However, the wind is gone down and the sea a little smoother. Our provisions are delivered to us from the store-room on Mondays and Thursdays and our water every morning. This morning it was taken from a fresh cask, and it stank so that we could not drink it, so we were obliged to boil it and put peppermint with it. (Plate 12)

Tuesday 2nd:

The weather more favourable. Myself, Bat, and Prudence and the family have all slept well. I woke up this morning with my soul alive to the power and spirit of God, filled with more zeal for His glory and the salvation of my soul and of my fellow mortals.

> Jesus confirm my heart's desire
> To work and think and speak for Thee
> Help me to guard the holy fire
> And still stir up Thy gift to me.

Wed. 3rd:

Still continues fine. The vessel is sailing as easy as a steam carriage. I have slept so well as if I had slept in the Queen's chamber. It (is) delightful to view the surface of the great deep. Today our Ed. Fulford met with a loss: his cap went overboard. It cost 5/- (25p.), but Uncle Richard gave him another.

We have been in company with another vessel outward bound. She is so far off that we can only see her with the spy glass. We held our prayer meeting in the cabin.

Thursday 4th:

Continued fine until midnight: then the wind freshened and blew hard. We have now been one month at sea and are now near the Banks of Newfoundland. However, it is pleasant on deck today. We are making speed at the rate of 7 or 8 miles an hour. From 12 o'ck midnight till noon today we have sailed 84 miles.

Friday 5th:

Continued a fine breeze: favourable wind. This morning we discovered a number of sea-pigs[1], also a number of ice-floes. The Cap. ordered the sailors to take soundings, which they did, but at 100 fathoms they could not find bottom: a fathom is six feet.

I did a job of work for the Cap. this morn. About noon a mist set in, then heavy rain, so the Cap. considered we were near the Banks of Newfoundland.

[Ship's masters aimed to find the edge of the Grand Banks by soundings and by the observation of fog and of the colour of the water, in the correct latitude for their destination. The master continued to take soundings to establish his position on the Banks. The same procedure was observed in the *Ocean Queen* (Thursday 3rd May) and much the same weather experienced.]

As is the custom, all on board that have not crossed the Banks have to pay their footing, so old Father Neptune came on board with a tar-brush, and piece of hoop-iron for a razor, to shave all who refused to pay. He first entered the cabin, demanding 1/6d. (7½p.) from the cabin passengers and 1/s. (5p.) from the steerage. If they refuse he executes their punishment. The money collected will be divided on arrival at Quebec, so that they may get themselves grog and have a spree.[2]

Sat. 6th:

Continued fine and very misty, but no misfortune through the ice. It is customary for the passengers to keep watch as we are in danger of running into ice, so four of the men have kept watch.

There are abundance of fish on the Banks. One of our sailors with a hook and line caught a large codfish, 17¼ lbs. It is now so cold that I can bear the heat of my Chesterfield coat, and mittens on my hands, all day long. On taking soundings today the Cap. found the depth to be 39 fathoms.

---

[1] Dolphins of some kind.
[2] See page 8 and *Ocean Queen* journal for Wednesday 2nd and Thursday 3rd May.

Sunday 7th:

While on the Banks there are sudden changes, so the men passengers attend to their watch and their station is at the bow. At intervals they walk the deck and blow the horn if they see anything. I thought this morning of the priveleges and quiet of my native village of Buckland, of the class-meeting and Sunday-school and my dear classmates. S.S. scholars, you are all near my heart. I cannot forget you although three thousand miles away. Never have I proved the blessing of the class meeting so much as in the weeks which have passed since I assembled with you. I get a blessing while changing the tracts and talking with those that read them.

Just as we were retiring to rest the watch gave a signal: abundance of fish floating around the vessel. As it was moonlight they were beautiful to behold. They shone like silver in the water.

Tonight Ed. Fulford was on the first watch and John Fulford the second with two others, Mr Shute and the cook, Ed. Bale attended on behalf of Bat.

Mon. 8th:

Still misty and cold. This morning we saw a French fishing vessel at anchor. Their mode of fishing is to have a long line three miles long with hooks tied on at every fathom, a weight to each end to sink it, also a line at one end to come to the surface of the water with a buoy so that they can find it again. Their buoy pole stands upright with a flag on it. Our sailors launched the boat, went to a line and brought back thirty codfish: some of them weighed 30 lb. each.[1]

Tuesday 9th:

The weather changed; all clear; fresh breeze and fair. The Cap. changed our course as we were rather far north. Fine sailing: 7 to 8 miles an hour. Prayer in the hold at the usual time 7 o'ck.

Wed 10th:

No men passengers attended to watch tonight. Vessel clear of the

---

[1] The pious writer makes no comment on stealing fish from another man's line, perhaps he thought the French fair game.

Banks. Sailing 7 to 8 miles an hour and getting very near to land. Through the unchangeable mercies of God, myself, Bat, Prudence and all the family enjoy good health and strength of body, as do all the passengers on board.

This afternoon we have been in company with another fishing barque since the course of the day. Assembled this evening in the cabin for prayer.

Thurs. 11th:

Obscure mist and fog. Vessel making fair way: 7 to 8 miles an hour. No ice. In company with a vessel outward bound. The sea is much smoother and the vessel more steady. Done another job of work for Mrs Crealock of Littleham.[1] This morning at dinner time we saw a wild goose flying. This afternoon we have discovered a large sheet of ice, the first we have seen since we left the Banks. It was right ahead. The Captain gave orders to take down some of the sails and put the vessel in another direction. It is now so cold as in the depths of winter. Held our prayer meeting and commended ourselves to God.

Friday 12th:

Continued very rough in the beginning of the night till ten; the vessel rolling heavily then there came a sudden change and the sea became a little more calm. This morning the atmosphere is clear and the sun shining. At ten o'ck the Captain gave orders to turn the vessel about from the north to the south, and at 12 o'ck, to the joy of every heart we saw land, the island of Cape Britton.[2] We were within a distance of ten miles, right opposite the Gut of Cosen, where John Dennis of Buckland Brewer, sailed up on his way to Guysesborough in America.

The next land we saw was St Paul's Island, which we saw was covered with brushwood. There is a lighthouse on the island, the sole habitation there.

[Cape Breton Island, the most easterly part of Nova Scotia, is separated from the mainland by the Gut of Canso (not Cosen as

---

[1] Previously referred to as Miss Crealock. Mrs. was often used as a courtesy title.
[2] See William Gliddon, Thursday 10th May.

written above) through which vessels bound for New Brunswick and Prince Edward Island frequently sailed when conditions were right. Thinly populated, although its coal mines at Sydney were developed early in the 19th century, it remains today largely forest. The Cape Breton Highlands National Park in the north and the Cabot Trail are important tourist attractions. Guysborough, Nova Scotia, is on the mainland shore of the Gut of Canso. St. Paul's Island is about ten miles beyond Cape North. 'A Cabin Passenger' in 1847 described it as:

> '... a huge rock, dividing at top into three conical peaks. Rising boldly from the sea, there is a great depth of water all round it, and vessels may pass at either side of it. It has been the site of numerous shipwrecks; many vessels, carried out of their reckoning by the currents, having been dashed against it when concealed by fog, and instantly shattered to atoms. Human bones and other memorials of these disasters are strewed around its base.'

William Gliddon described two lighthouses on it in 1855, (Thursday 10th May). This is the true beginning of Jacques Cartier's 'goodly great Gulf, full of islands, passages and entrances, towards what wind soever you please to bend', within whose arms lies the crescent-shaped Prince Edward Island, 'garden of the Gulf'.]

We are now entering the Gulf of St Lawrence, and we have the Island of Newfoundland in view. We are in great peril of being crushed by the ice, which covers a distance as large as five parishes of Buckland. Fortunately it is broken, so that with great skill and care the sailors stand in turn with the Captain in the bough and give the signals to the man that is steering the vessel so as to pass through the ice. However, some of the ice floes strike the sides of the vessel, and knocked her motionless, sounding almost like thunder. This evening we saw a large whale spouting up water like a shower of rain.[1]

Sat 13th:

At 12 o'ck at night we met a large ice floe like a mountain: fifty

---

[1] A large whale here in the Gulf might well have been a Black Right whale.

feet wide, and twenty feet high. It passed very close to the vessel. We were hours passing it, but thank God we came to no damage. We thank God that we are the monuments of his mercy. This afternoon we saw seven whales skipping past us, taking their pastime in the great deep.[1]

Sun. 14th:

A dead calm. Another Sabbath at sea, and I bless God that he still inspires me with a sacred delight for the Sabbath. The cry of my soul is, 'Make me more useful and fruitful in every good work. May the Lord enable me to do so, for Christ's sake, Amen.' Changed the tracts and at 11 o'ck Ed. Cann gave an exhortation from the 19 Chap. Genesis: 'Escape for thy Life'. I pray that the seed sown may not be in vain. A refreshing day to our souls.

Mon. 15th:

Wind fair, with a brisk breeze. Vessel sailed 100 miles the night past and this morning. We are all well, thank God: myself, Bat, Prudence and family, William and Sarah Shute, J. Collins, Richard Nicols, and John Ancock. Bless God for it, as our joy is still increasing that we are very near Quebec.

We are in company with a great many vessels bound to Quebec. This morning we saw more land: St. Ann's Island. It seems like a mountain reaching the clouds, covered with snows. We held our prayer meeting in the hold.

Tues. 16th:

The wind has been contrary through the night and now is at a dead calm. A pilot from the Port of Quebec although we are still two or three hundred miles from it. The reason they come out so far is to prevent future evils. The pilot enquired of our Capt. how many tons of goods our vessel carried and from what port we came, what country, and who the passengers were, if we were in good health and had kept clean, and if our hold was white-washed. After the Capt. had shown him and satisfied him there was no diseases, the pilot appeared in a manner and deportment very orderly and

---

[1] Probably Minke whales.

circumspect and respectful. The luggage he took on board from his pilot vessel was a box, a bed, and changes of raiment; and Mr Heard must find him food and wages: so much per foot as the vessel's run in the water.

By day the pilot takes his place in front of the cabin and walks the deck, also goes down into the hold and examines our berths. By the Emigration Laws there are companies of these pilot men kept at Quebec, licenced by Government, provided with vessels to carry forty or fifty pilots from which they put one man into every ship that they meet.

Wed. 17th:

Wind still contrary with rough sea. The Capt. gave orders to change the vessel's course. This afternoon it became finer and the weather more clear.

Thursday. 18th:

The sixth week at sea. The wind changed fair. Vessel making good speed. At five o'ck we could see an extensive range of woodland and lumber land, not so high, with enclosed fields, a great many settlements with farms and dwelling houses. The land looks very fertile. We have seen uncultivated land enough to accommodate millions of the labouring class and population of England. It appears to me with some capital you may enlarge you borders.

Fri. 19th:

Through the course of the night the wind changed with heavy rain. This morning we arrived at Break Island, where the pilot took charge of the vessel so that for a hundred miles he will have the sailing of the vessel, and the sailors under his charge.

[This is undoubtedly Bic Island, the usual place for the pilot to take charge — see also William Gliddon, Wednesday 16th May. It is supposedly a mis-pronunciation of Pic (peak), the name given by Champlain on his earliest Quebec voyage in 1603.]

The passengers are busy in washing and cleaning their berths, the females are washing linen and performing laundry work, so that the inspection can be satisfactory to the doctors on the Quarantine Grounds when we arrive.

We are now in company with twenty to thirty vessels. This evening the pilot gave orders to cast anchor: the first time while on our voyage; also to reef the sails for the night, and so did all the other vessels, as the wind and tide were not brisk enough for them to sail.

Saturday 20th:

Two of the sailors remained on deck to keep watch. The remainder retired to rest until 5 o'ck when the pilot gave orders to draw up the anchor and set the sails with a flowing tide, and fair wind. The men passengers went on deck and gave a helping hand.

The *Spring Flower* from Padstow came in company with us.[1] She passed ahead of us this morning. We saw horses and cattle on the land this morning. During the course of the day we have seen hundreds of thousands of acres of land that is cultivated, with towns and villages which appear to have been enclosed and cultivated for fourteen or twenty years. We find by the sun that the time here is really five hours slower than England, so that when it is twelve noon, it is five in the evening in England.

Sunday 21st:

Continued fine. A fair wind. At half past seven this morning we arrived at Quebec Quaranteen Ground (Plates 16–21) which is thirty miles from Quebec.[2] We cast anchor, which is on the North side of the river. There is an English settlement and hospital under our Government, and doctors for the reception of sick passengers; but through the mercy of God it was fortunate for us: we were the most decent and healthy passengers the doctor has ever seen or examined. So we were detained only two hours. We weighed anchor and sailed up the river, which is the most beautiful scenery that can be seen.[3] We saw the waterfalls of Merance, which falls

---

[1] A brig of 225 tons, built at Sunderland in 1825, owned by Avery & Co of Padstow, voyage to Quebec 1848, Master, T. Richards.

[2] See accounts of Grosse Île, pages [12–13] and William Gliddon, Saturday 19th May.

[3] See accounts of this scenery on page [60], and William Gliddon, Sunday 20th May.

two hundred feet. (Plate 22) We arrived at Quebec Harbour (Plate 23) at 5 o'ck, and cast anchor, thankful to Almighty God for His persevering care through the space of six weeks and three days on our voyage. We assembled ourselves for the last time in the cabin and held a prayer meeting, praying that if we never meet more on earth, we may meet in Heaven.

Monday 22nd:

We have all slept well through the night. This morning at 8 o'ck another doctor came on board and examined us. We all passed his approval. Also the custom house officer took the number of passengers. We are now as busy as bees packing our baggage to go on board the steamboat: myself, Bat, Prudence and family are bound for Montreal, and the fare is 4/- (20p) for adults and 2/- (10p) for children. From Montreal to Kingston is the next place (Plates 24, 25) we are bound for. We find it as great a trial to part from our fellow passengers and acquaintances as it was to leave friends in England, as the Captain and sailors were very kind and good to us all. I do not regret leaving England, as I feel I am still in the way of the Lord. I have now to acquaint you that I received as a gift from Mrs Crealock a number of *The Cottager's Friend* of the November month dated 1837. Opening it at page 155 I find it gives an account of the introduction of Wesleyan Methodism in Bideford and Buckland Brewer, and as Mr Barth Fulford, Wesleyan Minister of Buckland Brewer often asked me if I had seen any account of such publication, I have now enclosed it with this journal and sent it from Quebec to them in hope that it will be satisfactory to his wishes.

And now, my dear brothers, sisters and relatives and all enquiring friends, myself, Bat, Prudence and the children send our kind love to you all, hoping it will find you enjoying good health. At present we have reason to bless God for it. Wm. Shute and Sarah sends their kind love to their parents, especially to his brother, Ricky and John and Mary Ann and Mary Jane Heard; and be sure to give Uncle Billey's kind love to Ricky. Tell him that Ching and Smokey-pipes and Sarah is in good health in America. Also John Collins sends his love to C.C., a particular friend, and all his enquiring friends.

I hope that you will excuse bad writing and mistakes and blunders, as I have had much difficulty in writing on this voyage, through the rolling and tossing of the vessel.

I send this Journal first to John and Jane Mills at Northam, and beg that you will favour John and Elizabeth Fulford, Rebecca Davidson, Thomas and Mary Ann Cook with the perusal of it; and that John Mills will have the kindness to send or carry it to Robert and that Sister Taylor will favour mother-in-law, Maria, Sam, and Betsey Bray, Mr Hookway and Mary Jane, Mr Oatway and Christianna, Mr Pridham and Susan, Mr and Mrs Mathews, also Mary Hate. They all will have the perusal of it, and I beg that Sister Taylor will have the goodness to send it to Buckland Brewer to Brother John and Grace Fulford; and Susan Fulford will convey it to John Rowe who will convey it to Mr Barth Fulford who will have the goodness to send it back to Bideford, to Mr Robert Taylor on the Quay, after you have all read it.[1]

So now, my dear Friends, I must conclude my Journal hoping that if we never meet on earth we may all meet in Heaven.

I remain your affectionate Brother and Friend.
Wm. FULFORD

[1] Mr S. I. Fulford, who farms near Buckland Brewer says that the Fulfords were all keen Wesleyans and that Bartholemew was a lay-reader. *White's Directory*, 1850, lists him as a farmer. Southwood House, Uncle Billie's 'Residence and Birthplace', though much altered is still a farm in the centre of Buckland Brewer. Although less than a dozen miles from Bideford, the village is still deeply rural and except on the Bideford side can be approached only through the narrowest of Devon lanes. (Plate 6)

PLATES

Plate 1 This photograph taken in Ireland in the second half of the last century has a note written on the back, 'Peter Kelly aged 94 when this was taken'. It shows a way of life vastly inferior to the standard of living made possible by successful emigration and compares unfavourably with the homesteads in plates 29 and 30. (National Maritime Museum)

Plate 2 The prospective emigrant often had little to lose. Life on board a sailing vessel was no worse than life in the cottages, such as this one on the Isle of Skye, from which many of them had come. (*Illustrated London News*)

Plate 3 These coasters alongside Bideford Quay circa 1860 and other deepwater vessels were familiar to the people from the inland villages who visited the town on market day. (National Maritime Museum)

Plate 4 'The ship *Civility* left Bideford Quay at 7 o'ck in the morning and sail'd down the River to Appledore...'
It was from this bridge over the Torridge at Bideford that so many thousands waved farewell to their emigrant friends and relations. There is a barque at the quay below the bridge with her topgallant yards sent down. Appledore is at the mouth of the river, due North on the left bank but round the corner. (National Maritime Museum)

Plate 5 The *Civility* was smaller but otherwise very similar in appearance to this barque, the *Alma*, 356 tons, built in 1854 at New Bideford, Prince Edward Island, for James Yeo. (the late Kenneth Richards, Charlottetown).

Plate 6 The centre of Northam in the 1860s with the farm right on the village street gives a good impression of a big North Devon village at this time. Southwood House, the farm in Buckland Brewer from which William Fulford came, is similarly situated. (Bideford Museum)

Plate 7 *Civility* and *Ocean Queen* both lay off Appledore quay and were visited by their owners before going out over the Bar. This photograph of Appledore quay was probably taken in the 1860s. The vessels are the smack *Happy Return*, built at Fowey in 1846, and the schooner *Countess of Caithness* of Wick, built at Garmouth in 1856. (National Maritime Museum)

Plate 8 William Yeo, 1812–1872.
'About half past four we got under way with a good breeze, having on board a fine crew of twenty, Mr Yeo (the owner), the pilot, 22 passengers, a pig, a cat, and a dog.' (The late Collingwood Yeo, Prince Edward Island).

Plate 9 One fact alone made possible the cheap passage of vast numbers of emigrants. This was the arrival in England of vessels laden with timber from Canada. This photograph shows the 'tween decks of a timber ship with a partially stowed cargo of squared timber. There are no known photographs of accommodation in an emigrant vessel but this one shows the space in which their bunks and benches would be built. On the return voyage to England it would once again be filled with timber. (Nottman Collection)

Plate 10 'Today we have been visited by about 500 people who came on board to see the ship that is intended to carry us across the wide Atlantic ...'
This harvest jug commemorates the *Ocean Queen* and is witness to the pride and interest taken in the locally-owned vessels. (Bideford Museum)

Plate 11 'All the passengers are better, getting their appetite and complaining of their hunger.' Emigrants at dinner. (*Illustrated London News*)

Plate 12 'Our water is delivered every morning. This morning it was taken from a fresh cask, and it stank so that we could not drink it, so we were obliged to boil it and put peppermint with it.' Emigrants collecting boiled drinking water. (*Illustrated London News*).

Plate 13 'The Captain desired me to collect all the children that were fit for tuition and teach them to read and spell, two or three hours a day.'
A group of emigrant children having a reading class. Other emigrants are sunning themselves and airing their bedding, whilst others with buckets are drawing their water ration. (*Illustrated London News*).

Plate 14 'This fore noon whilst myself and several passengers were in the cabin the Capt. kindly took out the chart and pricked off every day's work, that we might see the course we have made.' (*Illustrated London News*)

Plate 15 'We finished up this week with a good dance'. (*Illustrated London News*)

Plate 16 'Weighed anchor about 3 a.m., reached as far as Quarantine Ground and anchored ... About 10 a.m. the doctor came off in his gig, rowed by four men.'
This is the western end and landing place on Grosse Île in 1832. Notice the

'telegraph' or signal pole on what is still known as Telegraph Hill. A brig is at anchor in the Quarantine Ground, flying signals to identify herself on arrival and her crew are making fast the sails. A steamer is coming down from Quebec, other vessels are bound towards Quebec City and boats in the foreground are going to and from the anchored vessels. This drawing was made by Captain Alderson who was in charge of the battery (Plate 20). (Public Archives of Canada)

Plate 17 'By means of the Capt's glass we can see a big fellow with a rake and a pair of tongs turning over the clothes and making the people clean them. They are scattering about the island, washing and scrubbing like fun: It is a very pretty island.' Cholera Bay, Grosse Île, – it was here that William Gliddon saw the emigrants washing their clothes. Beyond the beach one of the buildings where those administering the quarantine station lived now lies empty. (Basil Greenhill)

Plate 18 View in 1978 looking eastwards from the granite cross on Telegraph Hill. The anchorage from which Captain Alderson made his sketch (Plate 16) is off the end of the pier in the middle distance. (Basil Greenhill)

Plate 19 The Valley of Death – the only place where the soil was deep enough to bury the dead. The plain wooden crosses are visible, tip-tilted above the wild michaelmas daisies. The photograph is taken from the monument to the four doctors and '5,294 persons, who, flying from pestilence and famine in Ireland in the year 1847, found in America but a grave'. William Fulford arrived at Grosse Île during the following May but made no reference to the disaster of the previous sailing season. (Basil Greenhill)

Plate 20 The battery of three guns set up under Captain Alderson's command to control the deepwater channel between Grosse Île and the southern shore of the St Lawrence river. (Basil Greenhill)

Plate 21 Hospital buildings erected at the eastern end of Grosse Île in the early 1850s and used as an isolation unit. They would have been new at the time of the *Ocean Queen*'s passage and were used during the Second World War to house hens. (Basil Greenhill)

Plate 22 The Montmorency Falls were mentioned by almost all travellers up the St Lawrence. This painting by Robert C. Todd (active 1834–65) shows the ice cone which forms at the base of the falls in winter. (National Gallery of Canada)

Plate 23 This water-colour by M. M. Chaplin of 'Quebec and the coves from Point á Piso' shows timber rafts lying in the river waiting to be loaded into sailing vessels. (Public Archives of Canada)

Plate 24 To continue up the St Lawrence from Montreal it was necessary first to by-pass nine miles of rapids. From Lachine one travelled by bateau. This one, carrying a company of soldiers, is shown *descending* the Lachine rapids. It was painted by H. F. Ainslie in 1843. (Public Archives of Canada)

Plate 25 This steamer, the *Great Britain*, painted by H. F. Ainslie in 1839 at Kingston, Ontario, made journeys from Prescott to Niagara and back every five days. (Public Archives of Canada)

Plate 26 'Walls formed of straight logs – rough and undressed, laid horizontally crossing each other at the corners of the building, coarsely grooved or notched about half through so as to allow each log to touch that immediately below it ...' This water-colour by W. H. Bartlett shows a clearing in the woods where settlers have begun to build a house. (Public Archives of Canada)

Plate 27 'There cannot be a more extreme contrast to any country that has been long under cultivation ... than the boundless forests of America. An emigrant set down in such a scene feels almost the helplessness of a child.' White pines growing in Prince Edward Island. (Basil Greenhill)

Plate 28 A virgin forest is an ugly place with ancient trees fallen against young ones, with jagged stumps sticking up out of swampy ground where previously there has been a fire. This forest is in King's County, Prince Edward Island. (Basil Greenhill)

Plate 29 'He must build his own house, construct his own cart.' The settlers in this water-colour by P. B. N. Bainbrigge have cleared a reasonable area and appear to be quite prosperous. (Public Archives of Canada)

Plate 30 Meacham's *Atlas* shows many a tidy little homestead. This is a typical scene in Prince Edward Island where many of the wooden farmhouses of the 1860s and '70s with their large barns and adjacent woodlots remain in use to this day. (Public Archives of Canada)

1

2

3

4

5

6

Northam Village.

7

8

9

10

11

12

13

14

15

16

17

18

19

20

21

22

23

24

25

26

27   28

29

30

Log Kept by William Gliddon

A young man from Barnstaple, during a voyage from Appledore to Quebec in the ship *Ocean Queen*, 1000 tons burthen, R. J. Dart, Commander.

[The full-rigged ship *Ocean Queen* (later converted to barque rig) was built in 1845 at New Bideford, Prince Edward Island, by William Ellis for James Yeo of Port Hill, P.E.I., who signed the Builder's Certificate. She was registered as of Charlottetown, P.E.I., 630 tons, 122.4' x 27.5' x 21.5', and transferred to Bristol, England, in the same year as owned 32/64ths by James Yeo and 32/64ths by William Yeo of Appledore, North Devon. She was owned by them until she was officially recorded 'foundered off Scilly 19.5.65'. Bound from Newport with coal for Halifax, N.S., she sprang a leak on 17th May, 1865 and was abandoned on 19th May. Her crew of eighteen were picked up by the barque *Hygeia* of South Shields bound Barbados towards London and were later put on board a Scilly pilot boat.

James Yeo, a weekly carrier from Kilkhampton to Bideford with a one-horse cart, emigrated to Prince Edward Island in 1819 to take charge of lumber extraction for a shipbuilding, merchandising and lumber business set up there by Thomas Burnard, merchant and four times Mayor of Bideford. (See also page [18]). He prospered and in the 1850s became the most important of the Island's shipbuilders and shipowners. He was also a merchant, landowner, banker and most powerful politician in the Colony. His eldest son, William, came back to Britain and established himself at Appledore as his father's agent – the reverse of the Heard family's arrangements. The Yeo house flags were a white Y on a red diamond for P.E.I. vessels and a red Y on a white diamond for Bideford of Bristol registered vessels, both on a blue background.]

We boarded the ship on Saturday March 31st 1855, between 4 and 5 p.m. Our first attention was to get the boxes arranged and lashed, and our beds made. There is something novel in making preparations for a home on board ship to those who have always been accustomed to land. It was a lovely evening, the moon shining brightly on the water, and in the distance was a large fire, caused by the burning of the gorse on Sandown End, forming a beautiful scene, such as could not be seen on shore. About 11 o'clock we turned in, with the idea of trying to sleep on the water for the first time in our new bedrooms, but we were all in too good humour to sleep, and jokes passed freely round amid shouts of laughter till near daylight.

Sunday, April 1st:

Today we have been visited by about 500 people who came on board to see the ship that is intended to carry us across the wide Atlantic, and to take their last farewell, previous to our leaving our native land. [Plate 10] 10 p.m. just as we are going below there is a boat hailed us, with two females from Bristol (passengers). They have come on board without bed, food, or scarcely anything to make them comfortable. However, arrangements are made for them tonight.

[The scene at Appledore had been described in the *North Devon Journal*, 1st March, 1855:

> 'OUR MERCHANT MARINE. – This gay maritime place is all bustle and activity, in fitting out shipping for foreign voyages. There are five large new ships, belonging to Mr Yeo, of this vicinity, getting ready with all speed – the *Ocean Queen* (advertised for taking emigrants), *Challenge, Crimea, Victory* and *Alarm*. It is a pleasing sight to see them all comfortably lying alongside the splendid quays recently built by the merchants of Appledore, in contrast with what it used to be a few years ago.' (Plate 7)]

Monday, 2nd:

Everything is ready for sea but we have no wind, so our expectations of sailing this morning are not realised. We have been ashore today with the two Passengers from Bristol to procure provisions, tinware, etc., for them. I have seen Mr. R. F. and sent home word that we are to sail this evening. About half past four we got under way with a good breeze, having on board a fine crew of twenty, Mr. Yeo (the owner), [Plate 8] the pilot, 22 passengers, a pig, a cat, and a dog. Half past five, the pilot has taken us safe over the Bar, and he and the owner took leave amid the cheers of all on board.

[It should be noted that the 'fine crew of twenty' were local men, many of them related, as was the case with the *Civility*, and none of them was over forty years of age. (see Appendices 1 and 2).

'Mr Yeo' was, of course, William Yeo, eldest son of James Yeo. He was living in Richmond House, now called The Holt, the mansion he had built overlooking Appledore and the river Torridge. He also built the Richmond drydock at Appledore and made a considerable fortune as a shipowner, merchant, landowner and banker. When he died in 1872 the prosperity of Appledore was badly affected. Richmond Bay, the scene of the Yeo family shipbuilding and merchandising in Prince Edward Island, was so named after Charles Lennox, 3rd Duke of Richmond, by Captain Samuel Holland, surveyor of the Island in 1764–5.]

The weather is beginning to look dirty: the wind is freshening and the sea is rising. Passengers are beginning to look queer and to 'shoot the cat'. We are just abreast of Lundy, and I am compelled to go below myself. There is a great difference between the first night on board ship and the first night at sea.

Tuesday, 3rd:

Strong breeze. I am confined to my bed and doing all in my power to turn my inside out.

Wednesday, 4th:

Strong breezes; still very sick, but I have managed to creep on deck for about an hour. We are now on the broad Atlantic with nothing but water and birds to look at. It is a grand sight to see the sea rolling so high and the ship riding it so gracefully.

Thursday, 5th:

Weather a little more moderate. I am able today to keep a little biscuit and coffee inside me. We sick folk have experienced great kindness from the steward, who has tended us with coffee etc., during our sickness. We have plenty of amusement on deck today in the shape of chess etc., and plenty of singing every day from the sailors; they sing every two hours, when they pump the ship out. It makes one laugh to hear some of their songs:

> 'And now my boys we're outward bound,
>   Young girls go a-weeping;
> We're outward bound to Quebec Town,
>   Across the Western Ocean'.

We have had a complete merrymaking below tonight, a sort of return of our first night's spree.

Friday, 6th:

Weather lovely. This is Good Friday, but we miss the people at the doors with the hot cross buns. This day is kept as a holiday by the sailors, just as if they were on land. I have seen the sun set this evening: it looks as if it were gone down into the Ocean.

Saturday, 7th:

Weather fine. I am just getting my appetite once more. I lost it when I came to sea but I guess I have just added it to somebody else's. We have now been on board one week, and know something about the Captain: he is a perfect gentleman, and his kindness to us is beyond anything we could ever have expected. We are just like cabin passengers; we go in and out as we like, and sit and chat and play drafts with him.

Sunday 8th:

Weather beautiful. This morning we have passed a bale of cotton, evidently washed off the deck of some ship. We have seen a whale[1] and a grampus; it is a great sight to see such huge monsters playing about in the water. We have also seen three ships today. There are no bells to be heard chiming, nor anything to point out Sunday from the other days of the week, except there is no work doing aboard.

Monday, 9th:

Weather fine, but head winds; so that we are not making much progress. Tonight we have had a concert below.[2]

Tuesday, 10th:

Strong breezes right in our teeth, scarce a stitch of canvas flying. Seen two ships, one passed almost close under out stern and we signalled with each other; they can talk by means of these signals just as if they were speaking to one another with their tongues. The first thing most commonly spoken is the longitude, then the ship's name, etc. There are ten different flags which answer the numerals; for instance every vessel has a number, and the Capt. has a book in which all the vessels' names are, with their numbers. The number of the *Ocean Queen* is 9085, and to show whether the number hoisted is intended for the name of the ship or for the longitude, there is always a distinguishing pennant hoisted over the name, and not over the longitude. There are several distinguishing pennants for various things, and these are exclusive of the ten which answer the numerals. There is a feeling on seeing another ship so close which cannot be described; you feel overjoyed to see other faces than those on board.

[The writer comments that ships most often enquired of each other the longitude, for this was the component of their position which was most frequently – and often fatally – wrong when a landfall was expected.

[1] Perhaps a Fin whale and a Killer, or some other large dolphin.
[2] 'Any person who can play the violin – the flute – the pipe, or any other instrument, becomes of interest and importance to the passengers, and is kept in constant requisition for their amusement'.
Illustrated London News, July 6th, 1850.

The code being used is Marryat and William Gliddon seems to have got it more or less right. In the 11th edition *(1851)* of Marryat's 'Code of Signals for the use of vessels employed in the merchant service' the *Ocean Queen* has the number 9085 under the first distinguishing pennant. (Marryat, being a naval man, spells the word 'pendant', but 'pennant' is the normal civilian spelling). In fact, Marryat makes use of ten numeral flags, a telegraph flag, a rendezvous flag, two distinguishing pennants and a numeral pennant, plus the merchant jack. Contrary to what is stated in the journal Marryat specifies that the numeral pennant is 'hoisted over a number when merely the figures are intended to be shown, and is hoisted between the numbers when the latitude or longitude is required'.]

Thursday, 12th:

Weather dirty – about 4 p.m. orders were given to close-reef all sails as a storm was expected; in half an hour every sail was furled and the ship pumped out, ready for the worst.[1] By this time the rain had begun to fall and the wind to rattle through the ropes like thunder. This lasted but a few minutes, and we were all in hopes it was past over easily, but as it got dark the rain again began to fall, the wind to whistle and the sea to rise. By ten o'clock the storm was getting hot. Thunder is no more than a dog's bark compared with the tremendous roar of the wind and sea. Ten o'clock all but three passengers went below, to turn in and try to sleep, and I being the hindmost left the scuttle open, thinking the other three would follow. We had scarcely turned in when a sea struck her, making her reel most awfully. It came down the scuttle like a millstream, washing some of us nearly out of our beds. Two of our boxes broke from their lashings and rolled about from side to side, strewing their contents as they went.

It was an anxious time: females shrieking, the water almost floating our things and the pails, cans, etc., knocking about. It is impossible to convey an idea of such an awful sight. We had very little sleep this night.

About 4 o'clock a.m. Friday there was a dead calm which lasted until about 7 a.m., when the storm recommenced with all its fury.

[1] See page [12] and William Fulford, Saturday 29th April.

The sailors on deck were obliged to be lashed, as they could not stand. We could cook nothing today, but the steward brought us some coffee, etc., and the Capt. comes down now and then to see us.

I went to the top of the steps this morning, just to see the sea. I never witnessed such a sight before; it was one mass of foam, rolling as high as our topmast, threatening every moment to swallow us up. About 2 a.m. another sea struck the ship, smashing in the cabin sky-light and some of the bulwarks. This completed the disaster of last night. We were now fairly washed clean out. This appeared to be the height of the storm, for it began to abate, and, thank God, by His aid we were carried safely through it.

Saturday, 14th:

The sea is again smooth, and we are engaged in getting our traps a little in applepie order once more.

Sunday, 15th:

The most beautiful weather we have experienced since we set sail. An American ship passed today, on her way to England.

Monday 16th:

Weather still lovely.

'Away, haul away, haul away, my dandies,
Away, haul away, haul away, Joe.'

When you come to 'Joe' you must pull. The crew leave work at 6 p.m., after which they amuse themselves and us, as they please. This evening they made their appearance on deck equipped as soldiers: they were capitally made-up: instead of a drum they had a tin box, and this greatly aided the burlesque. They marched aft to the cabin and one of the 'ossifers' handed the Captain a letter, the purport was that there was reason to suspect that one of their recruits was on board and that if he detained him any longer, he would have to take the consequences. The Captain gave them liberty to search the ship, and take him if they found him, which of course they very soon did; by this time two others of the crew had made their appearance equipped as countrymen. After some parleying of course they were enlisted and marched off to learn their exercise; not liking drill very well they ran away, and one was concealed in the long-boat, and when questioned as to the cause of his running off he answered that he 'ware towld to vall back, and he valled into the boat'. The other's excuse was that he 'went to see the maester he was gwine to live wi', when they 'listed en, but when he got the gate, he seed his *apprehension*, and he wur frightened'. This is only a specimen of the wit and humour displayed by the crew and I do not think any ship possesses a better crew.

Tuesday, 17th:

Weather foggy, but a pretty fair wind and running about six miles an hour. I ought to have said that after the storm we were only 70 or 80 miles off Cape Clear.[1]

Wednesday, 18th:

Weather dull and wet. Fair wind. It is amusing to sit on the rail after dark and watch the foam which the ship turns off as she cuts through the water, beautifully illuminated by a phosphoric light caused by the animalculae in the sea.

Thursday, 19th:

Fine weather and fair wind.

Friday, 20th:

Weather still fine. I made bread today which is allowed to be the best on board.

Saturday, 21st:

Weather fine, but strong breezes. Went 198 miles yesterday.

Sunday, 22nd:

Ditto weather. About 4 p.m. we passed almost close and spoke to

---

[1] Cape Clear – Clear Island, southernmost tip of County Cork, Eire.

the *Harmony* of St Johns, New Brunswick, bound for England:[1] shortly after a squall came on and we were compelled to furl our sails.

Monday, 23rd:

Weather squally, occasionally shipping a sea. We have a Wiltshire family on board, and I was rather amused at the following expression from one of them, 'Oi oit to hae cum 'ere az zoon az oi wur born to hae git rucked'.[2] Overtook two outward bounders today, as they are rolling most awfully. Our ship is as easy as an old shoe, and it takes a pretty considerable sea to roll her to any extent.

Tuesday, 24th:

Weather again fine, but becalmed till about noon when a fine breeze sprang up. This afternoon met the *War Eagle*, a new vessel from Saint Johns, New Brunswick.[3] She had lost her fore mast in a squall. We passed each other close enough to speak by word of mouth. Obliged to shorten sails again this evening: very squally.

Wednesday, 25th:

Weather still squally. Not making any progress. Have seen some Mother Careys Chickens or Stormy Petrels.

Thursday, 26th:

Weather fine, but wind dead in our teeth. Passed a large balk of wood completely covered with barnacles.[4]

Friday, 27th:

It has been a tremendous night, but this morning has brought a calm. This fore noon whilst myself and several passengers were in

---

[1] A schooner of 48 tons, built St. John 1845 by David Crandall. Sold to Belfast 1850.
[2] In west country dialects, ruck = rut, as wheel or cart rut; also a crease in a garment. Perhaps he meant 'get used to it'.
[3] A ship of 599 tons, built Nova Scotia, 1855, owner Meacock of Liverpool.
[4] These would be the stalked kind, the Ship barnacle, *Lepas*.

the cabin the Capt. kindly took out the chart and pricked off every day's work, [Plate 14] that we might see the course we have made, from the evening we sailed up to this morning. It is one of the prettiest courses imaginable: East, West, North, and South; backwards and forwards so that we have sailed more miles than would have fetched America, instead of which we are only 1200 from Lundy and 1750 from Quebec. The Capt. has never experienced such a continuance of foul weather. This evening we're encountering another storm.

[The 'day's work' was a method of recording the courses steered, (corrected for leeway, compass errors, etc.) and the speed the ship sailed (by the log chip and line). This was recorded on a traverse board or slate for each watch and the ship's position calculated at noon for each twenty-four hour period by working out the various courses steered and the speed sailed and combining these with the noon observed latitude. With contrary winds the ship's course over a period of weeks would look very complicated. For a full and simple account of the use of the traverse board, see Georg Kåhre's *The Last Tall Ships*, London, 1978.]

Saturday, 28th:

Weather delightful.

Sunday, 29th:

Weather fine, with a fair wind. This afternoon we have overtaken another vessel. We hoisted our ensign to see what countryman she was: up went in answer a French ensign. It is customary when answered to dip your ensign, that is, lower it half way, and raise it again; but the French are always more polite than we are: consequently they dipped to us three times. This evening we fell in with a shoal of porpoises.[1] It is quite entertaining to see them playing in the water, jumping over one anothers back etc. We are now in about the spot where the *Bellona* was lost last Spring. Our mate and carpenter was in her at the time. Yesterday we went 125 miles.

[It is not surprising that the *Bellona* was cause for comment. This

---

[1] General term for dolphins of some sort.

remarkable vessel sailed to and fro across the Atlantic often four times, occasionally even six times, a year for forty-one years. She was built in 1813 by Richard Chapman at Cleave Houses, Bideford, for Thomas Burnard, as a brigantine, 271 tons.[1] She was first used to carry troops and supplies to Bermuda during the War of 1812. She was converted to be a brig and finally re-rigged as a barque. Her last voyage is described in the *Islander*, Vol. 12, May 26, 1854, No. 598, under 'SHIP NEWS' thus:

> The Barque BELLONA, Pugsly, from Bristol, bound to Quebec, laden with iron, was fallen in with, abandoned, in lat. 34 or 36, one mast gone, her after part swifted up with chains, apparently having experienced heavy weather.

With such a dangerous cargo and with her hull wrapped around with chains, it was inviting disaster to send this venerable old vessel on a further trans-Atlantic passage.

The mate mentioned here is John Williams Dart, an Appledore man born in 1827 and probably a relation of *Ocean Queen*'s master Richard Dart. J. W. Dart's Certificate of Competency as Master, now in the National Maritime Museum, Greenwich, shows him to have served in *Bellona* as A.B.S. from Bristol–Quebec, February–September 51. For the fateful voyage of 1854 he was mate and the time served is given as two months. He was in *Ocean Queen* for 1 year 6 months. When his certificate was signed at Bristol on 26 March 1856 his total service at sea had been twelve years.]

Monday, 30th:

Weather dull, but fair wind. Speed about 8 or 9 miles an hour. This afternoon we passed over the Jacquet Bank. This evening our sails are again reefed.

Tuesday, May 1st:

Weather stormy. Speed about 7 or 8 miles an hour, with close-reefed sails. Nice fun in stormy weather occasionally trying to walk and having a somersault over the boxes.

---

[1] See page [18].

Wednesday, 2nd:

Weather fine. Expect to be on the Banks of Newfoundland tomorrow. It is customary on crossing the Banks, as on crossing the Line, for Neptune to come on board and initiate those who have never crossed before by giving them a clean shave.[1] About 8 p.m. the ship was hailed by Neptune and the following questions put: What ship? Where from? Where bound? Any of his sons on board? How many? On these questions being answered he bade us goodnight, and promised to come on board with his wife tomorrow about noon, if all was well, and then returned to the deep.

Thursday, 3rd:

Weather fine, but we appear to be in a different climate for it is piercing cold. There are plenty of Ice Birds[2] and Newfoundland Boatswains[3] flying about, and a large number of whales and porpoises playing around us in the deep. We are now on the Banks of Newfoundland. At noon we met an iceberg which made it still colder; it was about (as near as could be guessed) sixty feet above the sea, seventy feet wide, and two hundred in length. This was indeed a splendid sight as the sun was shining on it brilliantly which added greatly to its grandeur. Took soundings in thirty fathom of water. Received a note from the crew of which the following is a copy:

May 3rd, 1855.

Gentlemen and Ladies—
I have took the liberty of sending you these few lines to let you know that we have join together in friendship and unity between ourselves to set up a bit of amusement, which I hope you will support as far as your ability will allow you to, as we shall not intrude on you. If you give it with your free will it will be greatly acceptable, as we shall be glad to drink each of your health before we part from each other in Quebec, and if you do give anything you are at liberty to come on deck and see the

---

[1] See comments and footnote, page [10] and William Fulford, Friday 5th May.
[2] Probably Fulmar petrels, which are abundant on the Newfoundland Banks.
[3] The Arctic Skua, which chases other sea-birds until they disgorge their food, which the skua catches and eats, hence the Latin name *Stercorarius parasiticus*.

performance go on, and if you do not give anything you have better stop below, for if you come on deck you must take what is going, and if it is fine weather Neptune will be on board this afternoon, to visit all of you, and if it is not we must postpone it until it is better weather; and if anyone gives a little trifle let them enter their names, by doing so you will greatly oblige the Jack Tars of the *Ocean Queen*.

The amount subscribed was 8/s, (40p.), for which we received the following receipt:

> Ship *Ocean Queen* May 3rd, in the year of Our Lord 1855 – This is to certify that I, Neptune, King of the sea, have come on board of the ship *Ocean Queen*, at 3 p.m., and received of the emmigrants the sum of 8/s; this being their first visit to the Banks of Newfoundland going to Quebec in America.
> Signed, Neptune, King of the Sea;
> F.G. Secretary, on behalf of the emmigrants.

The Capt. gave them the afternoon for the spree, and about 3 p.m. Neptune hailed the ship and came on board. The procession proceeded from the fore-castle to the quarter-deck in the following order: Neptune and his wife in a tub drawn by four constables; then the doctor, then the barber, then the boy with the lather-pot, followed by a lot of constables, etc. Neptune was dressed as if in sea-weed; a long beard and moustache, a helmet on his breast, stuck full of nails, points outward; he carried in his hand a harpoon with a fish. His wife's dress was a very funny one. The doctor had his face painted, and carried before him a box containing his physic. The barber had his pole stuck in his hat, and his razors stuck in a belt round his waist. These were of very large dimensions and made out of old hoop iron: in fact the whole presented an appearance that would have done justice to any stage. Having reached the quarter they sang a song, after which the barber read aloud the Act of Parliament authorising the visit of Neptune with his suite, to initiate the novices. Neptune and his wife then left the car, came forward, and spoke to the audience and then all proceeded to 'midships to commence operations.

Neptune ordered the oldest of his children to be brought forward, two constables led him out blind-folded. Neptune told him to 'come and kiss his father', but of course he could not see and his face was run against the helmet of nails. The doctor was told to examine him to see if he was in a fit state to undergo the operation. This he did by feeling his pulse, administering a large pill and a draught of salt water out of one of his bottles; he was then pronounced fit.

The barber next took him in hand, put a large swab over his shoulders, well lathered his face with grease and tar asking him questions all the time. Every time he attempted to answer, bob went the brush into his mouth. The large razors were then scraped over his face and the operation concluded with the capsizing of a bucket of water over his head. There were four served in this manner, after which *Rule Britannia* was sung. This ended the sport, and Neptune and his wife again returned to the deep, wishing us all success on our voyage.

After they had changed their dresses and got right the Capt. ordered all the crew aft and regaled them with brandy; and the crew finished it all by giving three hearty cheers for their worthy commander and officers. Each of us then went into the cabin and took a glass of brandy with the Capt.

By this time fog had set in, men had to be stationed to look out, and the fog-horn to be blown as a signal to other ships. The fog is so thick that we can scarcely see the length of the ship.

Friday, 4th:

Continuance of the fog and fog-horns. Soundings taken at noon in fifty-fathoms.

Saturday, 5th:

Continuance of fogs. We're now about 210 miles from the island of Saint Pauls. We have a fair wind but we are obliged to sail cautious to prevent running into other vessels.

Sunday, 6th:

Still foggy and dirty. Plenty of whales blowing around us.

Monday, 7th:

Another winter; the snow is falling thick and fast and a bitter gale of wind is blowing dead against us.

Tuesday, 8th:

A strong gale has been blowing all night, but this morning the sun rose in all his splendour: despite this a sad gloom is cast over our ship. About a quarter to eleven one of the crew was told to go out (along the bowsprit) and loose the jib, but he being occupied at the time in repairing his clothes, another man offered to do it for him. He ran away out for that purpose, but by some misfortune lost his hold and was precipitated into the water. There were only one or two on deck at the time, but the alarm was instantly given, 'A Man overboard!' and everyone rushed on deck. Ropes and the lifebuoy were thrown to him, but he appeared insensible, and could not lay hold of any of them.[1] The Capt. gave orders to back the ship and man the boat, but before this was done the poor fellow was gone. I saw him for some time. It was the first time I ever witnessed a man drowning, and I hope it will be the last. There was a heavy swell on at the time, and sometimes we would lose sight of the boat altogether between the seas. The boat returned in safety to the ship, but without poor Isaac Harvey! His loss was deeply felt by all on board, and especially by the Capt. He was the support of his mother, who is a widow. The money which we subscribed for the crew to spend in Quebec they handed over to the Capt. for his mother.

It was very singular that it was the same man who had acted as Neptune; little did he think, nor did any of us, when he said, 'I must now return to the deep', that he would so soon be there in reality! This afternoon we spoke the brig *Bowes*[2] of Workington bound for Quebec, 34 days out. The sun set in his utmost brilliancy this evening, and the sky was beautifully tinged with

---

[1] The Labrador current causes the ocean here to be extremely cold. The vessel had been experiencing typical 'Banks weather' for a week. See page [62–63] for another account of this incident.

[2] A brig of 265 tons, built Workington, 1808, voyage to North America, 1855, owner Holliday, master J. Ellgood.

a rich green, a colour I never recollect seeing in the sky in England.

Wednesday, 9th:

The snow is again falling in real earnest, and the ship has a pretty effect, with the deck, spars, yards, sails, etc., all clothed in white. This afternoon we fell in with a brig from Carlisle, having passengers on board. They appeared over-joyed at the sight of another vessel, for they waved their caps, handkerchiefs, etc., in the air until we again distanced each other.

Thursday, 10th:

We are highly gratified by the view on deck this morning. We are almost close to the land: a portion of the island of Cape Breton named Cape North:[1] the first sight of land since we left Lundy. It is covered with snow and looks very pretty. About 4 p.m. we passed the island of Saint Pauls, which forms one of the entrances to the Gulf of St Lawrence.[2] There are two light houses upon it: a fixed light on the North side and a revolving light on the South.

Friday, 11th:

Plenty of snow and a strong breeze.

Saturday, 12th:

Weather fine. In sight of the island of Bonaventure and Cape Gaspé. The island is barren, but it looks pretty now it is covered with snow.

[Bonaventure Island, six miles in circumference, is three miles offshore. Named by Cartier, who landed there in July 1534, for St Bonaventure whose feast day is 4th July, it is now an important bird sanctuary. It can be reached by boat from Percé, the place of the spectacular pierced rock, south of the Baie de Gaspé. Gaspé town is at the head of this huge natural harbour and Cape Gaspé, a

---

[1] See William Fulford, Friday 12th May. Cape North is the most northerly point of Cape Breton and still not accessible by road.
[2] See William Fulford, Friday 12th May.

narrow limestone finger, emerges from the north of the harbour to become the most easterly point of the Gaspé Peninsula. The area is a National Park of great natural beauty and interest. The word Gaspé is said to derive from Gaspeg, meaning Land's End.]

We have plenty of ships in company now. This evening about 7 o'clock the pilot-schooner came alongside, and left us a pilot. We finished up this week with a good dance. [Plate 15]

Sunday, 13th:

Weather fine and a good breeze. Land in sight all day. The coast on the South side of the Gulf is very high and covered with snow.

Monday, 14th:

Weather dull and wet. Becalmed. Great amusement all day catching birds. There are hundreds about the deck. The Capt. shot a very large hawk, the Second Mate caught a small one, and the rest of us have caught dozens of blackbirds[1] and other kinds of small birds.

Tuesday, 15th:

Weather fine and headwinds. Land on both sides. On one side is Cape De Moats; on the other Cape St Annes and Cape Chatte. The Saint Anne mountains are a magnificent sight: the highest land in British North America, being 3973 ft above sea level. They are covered with snow. This evening we are becalmed and have had a splendid sight of the Aurora Borealis.

[This is the first – or last – point where one can see both shores of the St Lawrence. Pointe-des-Montes (called here Cape de Moats) is on the northern shore. Ste-Anne-des-Monts, on the southern shore was a place of pilgrimage which once prized a finger of its saint, a relic lost when the church was burnt. An outline in rock resembles a cat, but Cap Chat is probably a mispronunciation of Chatte (as given in the journal) or Chastes, and named by

---

[1] Not the English (European) blackbird but the American 'Rusty Blackbird', *Euphagus carolinus*, on migration from winter quarters in the south to nesting grounds in Canada.

Champlain in honour of a Lieutenant-General. The St. Anne or Shickshock Mountains are the extreme northern portion of the Appalachian system. The highest peak is Mont Jacques Cartier, 4,160 feet and thus higher than any summit in the Laurentians, it is the highest point in Quebec and a useful landmark for fishermen in the Gulf.]

Wednesday, 16th:

Weather dull wind fair. About turn made Bic Island,[1] where the pilot takes charge of the vessel. This is 150 miles from Quebec. 8 p.m., the weather has come on so thick that we are obliged to anchor. The River Saint Lawrence is one of the most dangerous in the world to navigate being so full of islands and rocks.

Thursday, 17th:

Weather fine. Weighed anchor. Scenery all along the shore magnificent, studded with houses all painted white, with here and there a spire rising above the rest. Between this and Quebec there is a church every seven miles. Passed Red Island: this is a pretty little island with only one house on it. We have also passed today, White Island and Brandy Pots, which is another small island with only one house on it. About 6 p.m. we reached the River de Loup. Here there is a telegraphic station; our name (signal) was hoisted and will be telegraphed to Quebec this evening, so that tomorrow the report will be forwarded to England.

[The *Ocean Queen* will have made her number (9085) in Marryat's code. The telegraph line to Quebec was no doubt electric by this date but there was no trans-Atlantic cable yet and the report would be forwarded from Quebec in the next vessel bound for England. Riviére du Loup, now an important railroad centre, was the place where Champlain first saw the Loup Indians, the Wolf tribe.]

Friday, 18th:

Weather lovely. Got through Traverses and then dropped anchor.

---

[1] See also William Fulford, Friday 19th May.

Having no wind we are obliged to drop anchor every ebb tide, and weigh again to drift when the tide is running up. It flows five hours and ebbs seven. There is always a very strong current setting down the St. Lawrence. Quite a fleet is lieing at anchor here. The scenery is very beautiful. About 1 p.m. we weigh anchor again and got through the Pillars, which are a lot of rocks or islands rising out of the river and leaving only narrow openings for navigation. This evening there was a mock auction held: we must have amusement of some sort.

Saturday, 19th:

Weighed anchor about 3 a.m., reached as far as Quarantine Ground (Plates 16–21) and anchored.[1] Here we must stay till we have got our certificate and have been visited by the doctor. Our signal was hoisted, and at about 10 a.m. the doctor came off in his gig, rowed by four men. We were all summoned on deck and ranged before him like a lot of soldiers about to be drilled. He gave us a clean bill, and we are allowed to proceed.

There are two ships lieing close in to the island; their passengers are fetched ashore to undergo a cleansing process. There are about 300 of them ashore, and by means of the Capt's glass we can see a big fellow with a rake and a pair of tongs turning over the clothes and making the people clean them. They are scattering about the island, washing and scrubbing like fun: it is a very pretty island.

About 2 p.m. one of the Quebec steamboats came down to Grosse Island with provisions for the Quarantine Station, and seven others came down this afternoon to tow up vessels, as there was no wind. One of them, the *John Bull* came alongside and wanted to tow us up.[2] He wanted eight pounds but the Capt. considered the charge exorbitant and would not give it him. It is only 30 miles from Quebec. We did not get above a mile next tide, and were compelled to anchor again; shortly after which a strong breeze sprung up, but it being dark, the pilot would not venture to weigh anchor.

[1] See pages [12–13] and William Fulford, Sunday 21st May.
[2] These steamboats also took emigrants up to Montreal from Quebec. The Quebec Gazette, 19th May, 1834, notes: 'The *John Bull* took up more than six hundred on her last trip.'

Sunday, 20th:

We weighed anchor about 4 a.m. and proceeded. The Island of Orleans which bounds the North Coast is a pretty island, and one mile below Quebec are the falls of Mont Morencai, about 60 feet high and 20 feet wide. I think the scene up the Gulf and River St. Lawrence repays all the expense and trouble of so long a voyage.

[See also William Fulford, Sunday 21st May.
The scene was well-described by *A Cabin Passenger* in 1847 and is much the same today.

> '... I had many near views of the southern bank of the river, and of the beautiful shore of Orleans Island, with its luxuriant orchards and well cultivated farms sloping down to the water's edge, and dark forest upon the crest of its elevated interior ... The magnificent Fall of Montmorenci then was revealed to view, in a sheet of tumbling snow-white foam set between the dark green banks, covered with fir and other trees ...[1]

The Montmorency Falls, 242' and thus a greater drop than Niagara but much narrower, were mentioned by almost all travellers up the St. Lawrence. They can be seen from Route 2 on the southern shore as one looks across the western tip of the Isle d'Orleans. Described in 1796 as 'altogether one of the most striking and pleasing scenes which this country affords', they have been drawn and painted many times. A painting in the National Gallery of Canada by Robert C. Todd (active 1834–65) shows the ice cone which forms at the base of the falls in winter. (Plate 22)]

We anchored in Quebec [Plate 23] harbour about 7 o'clock, and hoisted our signal for the doctor, for we are not allowed to go on shore nor put the vessel into the wharf before we have been cleared by the doctor and Custom House.

It has been blowing so strong a gale all day that no boat would be put off to board. Ships have been coming into the harbour all day: I should think there is about 100 sail here. The town or city of Quebec has not an imposing appearance; the houses are mostly of wood and painted every variety of colour. On every roof there is a

---

[1] Quoted in *The Great Migration*, Edwin C. Guillet, University of Toronto Press, 1963.

ladder so that in case of fire they can get onto the roofs easily. The Citadel looks very well, and I think it would be a teaser to an enemys fleet should one ever attempt to get into the harbour.

Monday, 21st:

Still blowing a gale, but the officer is out, and there are so many ships with their signals flying that we did not get a turn till 3 p.m. and as the Montreal steamers leave at 5.0 there is no time to get ourselves out of the ship and on to the steamboat so we must be contented for another day.

Tuesday, 22nd:

Still blowing heavily, and Capt. does not think it prudent to risk lives and property in the boats to get to the steamer; but some of our boxes we managed to get ashore so we were determined to go. Only a proportion of us, however, could leave, for after dinner it was blowing a hurricane, but we who had sent our boxes on board the steamer said we would go. The sailors at first hesitated about taking us ashore but we told them we were not afraid, and if they would wish to go with us, we would go. Accordingly we got into the boat and reached the shore in safety, although we had a thorough good ducking.

We left Quebec for Montreal at 5.30 p.m. in the *John Munn* and reached about 7.0 next morning; one hundred and eighty miles, for which we paid 3s. (15p.)

[The steamer *John Munn* was built at Quebec and first registered 31st May, 1847, 374 tons, 292' long, captain John Lockhart. She was one of several 'from the yards of Mr. John Munn and which cost their owner a part of his large fortune, so much so that Mr. Munn was not able to remake this fortune and he died relatively poor.'[1] In July, 1847, she had 'landed four hundred emigrants in a sick & dying condition, on the stone wharves', (at Montreal).[2]]

Montreal is a very pretty city and not at all like Quebec; there are a

---

[1] *The Construction of Ships at Quebec and District*, Part Two, by Narcisse Rosa, printed by Leger Brousseau, Quebec, 1897.
[2] *The Great Hunger*, Cecil Woodham-Smith, London, 1962.

great many handsome buildings and stores in it. The French Church is a fine building, and capable of holding 20,000 people. It has two towers, in one of which is the largest bell in the world, except one. These towers are 220 feet high.

Sunday, 10th June

On *Sunday, 10th June*, it was Procession Sunday, one of the greatest days in the year for the Catholics, when the houses of the Catholics in the streets which the procession would go through were trimmed with evergreens. Banners were flying from the towers of the Church and the bells ringing. About ten o'clock, hundreds of people were assembled in the front, with a view to getting a sight of the procession when one of the four pinnacles on one of the four corners of one of the towers fell off, and coming among the people, struck the foot of a boy, cut off his toes, and sank a considerable depth into the ground. Luckily this was all the damage done. Imagine a stone of sugar-loaf shape, six feet long, and weighing 183 lbs., falling from a height of 220 feet.

Just as the procession was forming it began to rain and continued heavily all day, so that I did not witness the great turnout, as I thought it would not repay for another wetting. Some of the children's dresses were studded all over with gold and silver spangles, just like mountie-banks; others again belonging to the nunnery were dressed in white, with a large piece of white lace covering their heads. They also had banners, bands, etc., etc.

[Here the Journal ends. The following account of the voyage was published in the *North Devon Journal* on 14th June, 1855:]

THE 'OCEAN QUEEN'. – This fine barque, which was fitted out in the most liberal manner, by the owner, Mr. Yeo, of Appledore, and sailed for the Western shores on the 2nd of April last, with a number of young persons of this town and neighbourhood, arrived in safety at Quebec, on Sunday, May 20th. The vessel encountered a succession of stormy and contrary winds throughout the voyage, and a melancholy catastrophe occurred off the Banks of Newfoundland. While one of the crew was employed on the jibboom, he fell off into the sea and, although every effort was made to save him, they were ineffectual, and, as one of the passengers expresses himself, 'it was dreadful to see that in a few minutes afterward a shoal of whales was playing round the vessel.' The uniform kindness of the captain and crew to the passengers was such, that before leaving the vessel an address of which the following is a copy, was presented to him:

'Quebec,
May 22nd, 1855.

To Capt. Richard Dart,
ship "Ocean Queen".
Dear Sir,

We, the undersigned passengers on board the ship "Ocean Queen", which has been so ably commanded by you during the voyage from the port of Bideford to Quebec, cannot take our leave of you without expressing our deep feelings of gratitude for the extreme kindness you have shewn us, and for your unremitting attention to render us all the ship could afford. We would also, through you, convey to the chief mate, Mr. J. Dart, the steward, Mr. D. Nicholls, and the ship's crew in general, our best thanks for the extreme kindness we have experienced from them.

(Signed). G. GRIBBLE,
W. GLIDDON,
W. KERSWELL,
F. GILBERT,
G. FLEMING,
R. MOORE, and others.'

A New Life in the Wilderness

It is a sadness that no letters survive from William Fulford or William Gliddon to describe how they fared in North America. Although not well-to-do, or they would have travelled as cabin passengers, they were both literate, adaptable and optimistic men with some practical or professional skills and perhaps some small savings. Thousands of Irish immigrants were not so fortunate. They would find that being destitute in the New World was no pleasanter than being destitute in the Old. The vessel they sailed in had provided them with a roof and with food for a few weeks – now they exchanged its wooden walls for the wooden sidewalks of Quebec, for a harsh climate, an unfamiliar language. Many of the poorest had no idea how to proceed. Some were lost as were the children in this advertisement placed in the *Montreal Transcript* in 1847:

> 'Information wanted of Abraham Taylor, aged 12 years, Samuel Taylor, 10 years, and George Taylor, 8 years old, from County Leitrim, Ireland, who landed in Quebec about five weeks ago – their mother having been detained at Grosse Isle. Any information respecting them will be thankfully received by their Brother, William Taylor, at this office'.

Many became a burden on the Emigrant Society of Quebec. For the rest, Quebec was but a staging post, not a journey's end. Many emigrants travelled further west, thousands poured down into the United States. Uncle Billie and William Gliddon both continued their journey by steamer to Montreal, where we lose sight of them. The former intended to go on to Kingston. To do so from Montreal it was necessary first to by-pass nine miles of rapids, by wagon or on foot. From Lachine one travelled by bateau:

'an open flat-bottomed craft about 40 feet long and 6 to 8 feet wide, usually constructed of pine boards. It was propelled by French-Canadians using oars, setting poles, grappling-irons, and a lug-sail or two, as conditions necessitated'. (Plate 24)[1]

One immigrant from Petworth described such a journey to Prescott, a town about two-thirds of the way from Montreal towards Toronto:

'Our travelling this way is very tiresome and took us eight days to get to Prescot: the first night we reached a village, and after begging hard we prevailed with them to let us lay on their floor: we carried our beds and slept there, at the charge of 6d. (2^1/$_2$p.) each: at break of day we went on board, and stopped at night where there was no house: we borrowed the sail, and as many as could get under it did; the others made a large fire, and sat or slept by it: the next day it rained all day, and at night we stopped at a village and prevailed with some poor people to lodge us, a house full, on their floor; they let us make tea and dryed our clothes: in the night I was taken ill with spasms, and a fever followed: I did not eat one mouthful of food for eight days: only drank a little port wine often. I could not hardly get in or out of the boat, nor did I think I should ever see Adelaide. We at last came to Prescot, sleeping on the ground every night but two: the boatmen were all Frenchmen, and no way obliging; we could not make the kettle boil by the fire. When we came to Prescot we were all very wet with rain, and went to a tavern, hoping to dry ourselves; but we were so many, standing in their way, they did not want us there, so we were forced to remain as we was.'[2]

The fact was, 'The population being panic-stricken at the havoc cholera was making, shut their doors on emigrants'.[3] Let us now look at the settler, arrived at the new land which he intends to clear.

'In Lower Canada the lands are disposed of in 50-acre

---

[1] *The Great Migration*, Edwin C. Guillet, University of Toronto Press, 1963.
[2] *Narrative of a Voyage of a Party of Emigrants, sent out from Sussex in 1834 by the Petworth Emigration Committee*. James M. Brydone, quoted in *The Great Migration*, Edwin C. Guillet.
[3] *Coburg Star*, July 4, 1832.

allotments and upwards; in Upper Canada smaller portions are to be purchased: the price in Lower Canada averaging 5s., (25p.), in Upper Canada 8s. (40p.), currency per acre. A settler is cautioned against trying what are called cleared farms from private jobbers. In most cases these cleared farms are quite exhausted ... Let him take the land for a year or two on trial before he purchases. The Government give frequently four or five years to complete a purchase.'[1]

Lord Selkirk, who organised two very successful settlements in Canada, one at Belfast, Prince Edward Island, and one on the Red river, Manitoba, wrote a fascinating book which describes the state of the Highlands and gives advice on emigration: (Plate 27)

> There cannot be a more extreme contrast to any country that has been long under cultivation, or a scene more totally new ... than the boundless forests of America. An emigrant set down in such a scene feels almost the helplessness of a child. He has a new set of ideas to acquire ... A detached and unsupported settler is liable, in the first place, to lose a great deal of time before he fixes on a situation ... most of the people who begin on new and untouched land, are reduced to a situation of more than savage solitude ... Every time one leaves his hut, he is exposed to the danger of being bewildered and lost ... in every work he has to perform, he is unpractised ... he must build his own house, construct his own cart, [Plate 29] and make almost all his own implements ... Winter may overtake him with his house unfinished, or, when completed, he may find it insufficient to resist the rigours of the season ... If illness attack him in his solitary residence, remote from medical assistance, his deplorable situation may easily be imagined ...[2]

A virgin forest is an ugly place with ancient trees fallen against young ones, with jagged stumps sticking up out of swampy ground were previously there has been a fire (Plate 28). The trees which could provide the settlers with wealth were also their implacable enemy. Lord Selkirk puts it in stark terms:

[1] *Illustrated London News,* July 6, 1850.
[2] *Observations on the Present State of the Highlands of Scotland, with a View of the Causes and Probable Consequences of Emigration.* 1805. Earl of Selkirk.

His awkwardness, too, exposes him to frequent accidents; the falling of the trees ... often takes a novice by surprise. To cut down the trees is but half the work; in destroying them, and preparing the land for the seed, a number of minutiae must be attended to; if from want of experience these are omitted, the consequences may be fatal to the crop ... Thus, independently of the accidents of seasons ... and over and above the danger of losing his seed-time altogether, by not having his land ready, the new settler has to add many chances that, from his own ignorance and mismanagement, his crop may totally fail.

Walter Johnstone, a self-appointed Scottish missionary in Prince Edward Island, wrote of the settlers in a letter home:

'whatever was the cause of drawing or driving them hither, they are all here placed on a level, and taught one lesson, namely, *that if they wish to eat, they must work.*'[1]

He described the essential clearance work in detail:

New settlers begin to cut down the wood where they intend to erect their first house. As the trees are cut the branches are to be lopped off, and the trunks cut into lengths of 12 or 14 feet. This operation they call junking. Thus, when the space intended to be cleared is cut down, junked and all lying in a promiscuous manner, fire is applied to it and if the fire runs well the greater part of the small branches will be consumed, but the trunks will only be scorched. These are next rolled together, made up in piles ... The stronger part of the family then go on to make up more piles, while the weaker set fire to those which are prepared ... After the wood is all burnt, the stumps are left standing about two feet high, scorched black with the first burning ... The people then begin planting their potatoes ... when the time for planting arrives, man, wife, children, and all that can handle a hoe, must work, as the season is short; and if the crop is not got in, want may stare them in the face, when a supply will be difficult to procure, and when there will be nothing in their pocket to pay for it ... After a crop of potatoes has been taken next year, the same ground is sown with wheat and timothy

[1] *Journeys to the Island of St. John*, ed. by D. C. Harvey, Macmillan.

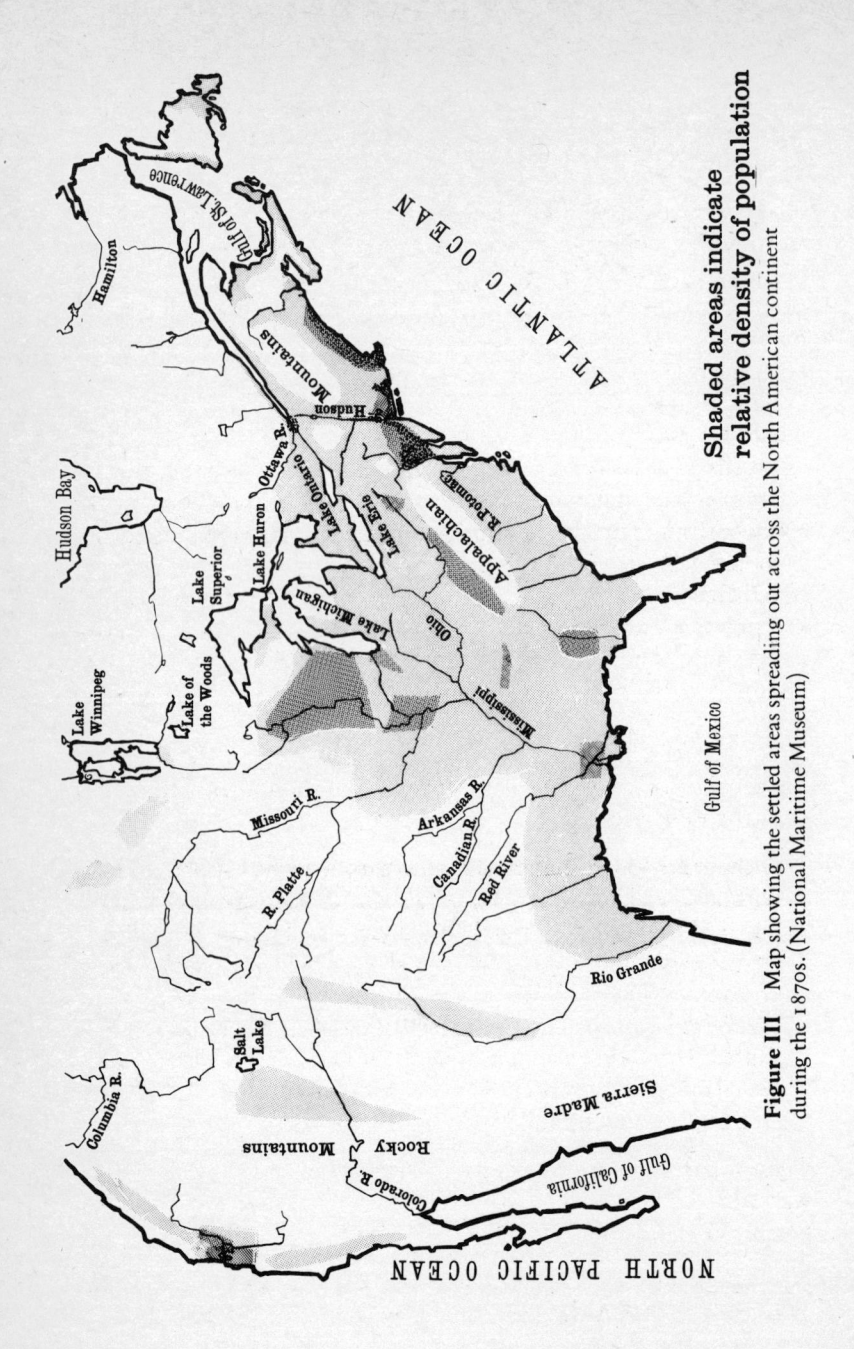

Figure III Map showing the settled areas spreading out across the North American continent during the 1870s. (National Maritime Museum)

grass seed ... After this, if the land is of a good quality, and has been well burnt, they can mow it several years among the stumps.

There were three methods of removing stumps after digging round them with grubbing hoes and cutting some of the roots. They could be raised manually by using levers, they could be pulled out by oxen or a stumping machine could be used, a high wooden tripod on wheels which had a tackle by means of which the stumps could be extracted like teeth.

Few settlers can have had any idea of the sort of winter they would have to face. They were wise to arrive as early in the spring as possible in order to prepare for it. Even so, they might find the snow still piled high under the trees in May. The thaw, too, was an awkward time, making it almost impossible to travel on dirt roads. Men between sixteen and sixty were conscripted in Prince Edward Island for four days every year to help with the making and upkeep of the roads. For all these reasons, the first generation of settlers might not clear more than twenty or thirty acres in their lifetime and the distant end of the farm would be carefully kept for firewood for future generations.

Lord Selkirk tells of the building of houses in three stages. First the people made temporary wigwams, like the Indians, then they constructed houses –

> without any other materials than what the forests afford, and without the aid of any tool but the axe. Walls formed of straight logs – 8" in diameter – rough and undressed, laid horizontally, crossing each other at the corners of the building, coarsely grooved or notched about half through so as to allow each log to touch that immediately below it (Plate 26) ... the chinks were stuffed with moss, clay, wedges of wood. The roof was of bark, peeled off in large unbroken pieces, secured by poles, tied down on them with wythes.[1]

These roofs kept out the rain – as protection from the sun they were thatched with acquatic grasses or with spruce twigs. If they prospered the settlers would build a better type of house on a

---

[1] *Observations on the Present State of the Highlands of Scotland, with a View of the Causes and Probable Consequences of Emigration.* Earl of Selkirk, 1805.

foundation of stone. They would make wooden shingles for the roof and boards for the floor; doors, windows, chimney and partitions would be executed with more care. This time 'some attention is bestowed on neatness and ornament.' The 1870 map (Figure 3) shows what had happened on the North American continent in the preceeding fifty years despite all the difficulties. People from other places than the British Isles had also arrived to fill the empty spaces, from Scandinavia, from Germany, from Holland, from France. They had found, as Mr. Johnstone had found Prince Edward Island,

> One entire forest of wood; all the exceptions to the truth of this literally are not much more, even including the present clearances, than the dark spots upon the moon's face.[1]

Fifty years later Meacham's Atlas shows many a tidy little homestead. (Plate 30)[2] Such a homestead belonged to the young farm servant whose letter was reported in the *North Devon Journal*:

> he has worked himself into a farm – not a hired one – but fifty acres of purchased land, to which ten more are to be soon added. Besides the land, there is the stock enumerating 25 bullocks besides other animals with the rest of the et ceteras of a farm. They had to be their own tailors, in the spring make their own candles and soap, etc.[3]

Suppose this couple had been married seven years ago in this country? asks the *North Devon Journal*.

> Where would have been the acres, the bullocks, the sheep, the corn, the candles, and the soap? Not only would there have been nowhere for them, but instead thereof hopeless poverty, dirt, drudgery, the Union, and a pauper's grave.

---

[1] *Journeys to the Island of St. John*, ed. by D. C. Harvey, Macmillan.
[2] *Illustrated Historical Atlas of the Province of Prince Edward Island*, from a survey under the direction of C. R. Allen, by J. H. Meacham & Co., Publishers, Philadelphia 1880.
[3] *North Devon Journal*, 16 April, 1857.

APPENDIX 1
Crew of the Civility

As recorded in the relative agreement for the voyage from Bideford towards Quebec March 1848.

		Age	Born	Wages	Last ship
Master	John Bale	37	Alphington, Devon	£6 per month	Civility
Mate	Richard Bale	26	Appledore	£4	Civility
2nd Mate	Edwin Bale	34	Appledore	£2	Augusta
Seaman	James Branton	28	Clovelly	£2	Henrietta May
Seaman	Thomas Dumnaltt	25	Braunton	£2	Roberta
Seaman	Richard Hutchings	33	Northam	£2	indecipherable
Seaman	Phillip Clibbert	23	Appledore	£2	Nightingale
Cook-steward	Edward Bale	34	Alphington	£2	Lord Ramsey
Apprentice	George Essery	18	Bideford	–	Civility
Apprentice	John Bradley	17	Clovelly	–	Secret

Ref: PRO BT 98/1517

APPENDIX 2

Crew of the Ocean Queen

Of Bristol as recorded in the relative agreement for the voyage from Bristol towards Quebec March 1855

Date of departure from Bristol 19th March 1855.

		Age	Born	Last ship
Master	Richard Dart	30	Appledore	*Ocean Queen*
Mate	John William Dart	27	Appledore	*Ocean Queen*
2nd Mate	George May	40	Northam	*Alma*, P.E.I.
Carpenter	George Gorman	30	Northam	*Ocean Queen*
Boatswain	Charles Pine	39	Braunton	*Susanna*, Bideford
Steward	David Nicholls	25	Appledore	*William Rennie*, Bideford
Cook	Thomas Lamprey	40	Barnstaple	*Susanna*, Bideford
Seaman	Thomas Keen	22	Appledore	*Telegraph*, Bristol
Seaman	Henry Williams	21	Appledore	*Hadsutt*, Bideford
Seaman	James Ford	21	Appledore	*Gem*, Bristol
Seaman	Isaac Harvey	24	Appledore (drowned at sea)	*Runo*, Dundee
Seaman	Edward Bate	37	Spaldin	*Worthy of Devon*, Bideford
Seaman	William Mayse	21	Dilford	*Billow*, Barnstaple
Seaman	William Jewell	39	Clovelly (put ashore sick 21st July at Bideford)	*Alarm*, P.E.I.
Seaman	William Prince	24	Clovelly	*Enterprise*, Exeter
Seaman	John England	18	Devonport	*Hope*, Bideford
Ordinary Seaman	William Rutherick	14	Appledore	*Victory*, P.E.I.
Ordinary Seaman	William Bassett	20	Appledore	*Rover*, Bideford
Ordinary Seaman	William Hare	18	Appledore	*Favorite*, Bideford
Seaman	Charles Darracott	22	Braunton	*Susanna*, Bideford

Isaac Harvey Net Amount due £1 1s. 4d. 1 chest sundries Date of arrival in Bristol, 26th July. The master remained, all others discharged.

Ref: PRO BT 98/4098

Typeset by Computacomp (UK) Ltd, Fort William, Scotland.
Printed in England for Her Majesty's Stationery Office
by Billing and Sons Limited Guildford, London, Oxford, Worcester

Dd 696311 K00